DERBY COUNTY
THE STORY OF A FOOTBALL CLUB

DERBY COUNTY
THE STORY OF A FOOTBALL CLUB

Anton Rippon

NORTH BRIDGE PUBLISHING

First published in Great Britain in 2013 by
North Bridge Publishing
20 Chain Lane
Mickleover
Derby DE3 9AJ

ISBN 978-0-9926779-0-9

Book design by Graham Hales, Derby

Printed and bound by Berforts Information Press Ltd

Contents

Introduction. 6

Acknowledgements. 8

Football in a Higher Order 9

Ups and Downs. 25

Enter Mr Jobey 37

The Penalty of War 47

Grateful To Be Playing Again 57

That Man Was Harry Storer 64

A Younger Man is Needed 71

"Brilliant ... that was Cloughie". 77

Mackay's Champions 93

"Good Luck – Whoever You Are". 100

"Just Wring Out My Shirt". 112

The Bald Eagle 130

Managers' Merry-go-Round. 139

An Unexpected Promotion 147

A Man Named Clough. 154

Introduction

I T WAS 20 December 1952 – my eighth birthday – when my father came home at lunchtime from the *Long Eaton Advertiser* and, as the fish and chips were being plated up, announced that we were going to the match. He'd already taken me to several reserve-team matches, but this was my big-time debut. That afternoon, Derby County faced Bolton Wanderers in the First Division. "Nat Lofthouse is playing for Bolton; it should be a good game," the old man told me as we finished our treacle tart and custard. The walk to the Baseball Ground was always the same: along Gerard Street, across Burton Road and up Mount Street, then Normanton Road, Harriet Street, through the Arboretum, left into Rosehill Street, down Malcolm Street (where householders stored bicycles for 3d for the afternoon) and into Colombo Street which led straight to the turnstiles for the Osmaston End of the Popular Side.

Just to confuse me, on the way was Molineux Street: I wondered if that was where Wolves played. Some years earlier, before I'd ever seen a live football match, I'd also been confused by a photograph that I'd seen in the *Empire News*. The caption said that it showed Chelsea playing at Stamford Bridge. But there was no sign of a bridge. Similarly, when I read that Fulham played at Craven Cottage, I'd conjured up an image of players weaving their way gently through a crowd of genteel ladies taking tea and cucumber sandwiches on a lawn. Anywhere that boasted a cottage seemed a strange place to play football.

Confusions aside, if the walk was the same as the one we took to watch reserve-team matches, the attendance was much bigger. The Rams Reserves would attract perhaps, 2,000 spectators to the Baseball Ground; on this day, as it turned out, there would be almost 13,000. That might still seem a small crowd by today's standards, but in 1952 Derby County were struggling, and this was the last shopping Saturday before Christmas.

It had been only seven years since the Rams had won the FA Cup at Wembley in the first post-war Final, but that fine team had gradually broken up and, despite twice breaking the British transfer record in the late 1940s, in the first year of Queen Elizabeth II's reign the team had dropped down the First Division table. The previous season the Rams had just about managed to stave off relegation and, by this December day, they had won only four matches of this campaign. I'd had my ears filled with tales of Raich Carter and Peter Doherty, and before them the likes of Sammy Crooks, Jack Barker and Dally Duncan. It was the memories of these names that now sustained supporters in such bleak times.

I'd like to say that I recall all the details of that match against Bolton but, of course, I was far too young to appreciate the game or the style of the players. I remember that Reg Harrison and the burly Jack Stamps, both of whom had gained Cup winners' medals with Derby at Wembley were playing because my father had pointed them out. And Bert Mozley, who had played for England in the Rams' better days, was at right-back. Another former England player, Jack Lee, was at centre-forward and scored a goal as Derby won 4-3. It was probably a real thriller; alas, I can't remember. Just as, although I can say that I saw Nat Lofthouse play, to be honest, I have no recollection of him. My only clear memory of that chilly afternoon is the smell: a heady aroma of Brylcreem and cigarette smoke.

Years later, through working with BBC Radio Derby, I would become good friends with Messrs Harrison, Stamps and Mozley. Jack and Norah Stamps would invite us to their golden wedding party, while Bert and Jean Mozley would one day show us round the beautiful Canadian city of Victoria. They had emigrated in 1955. I would also manage to play against Jack and Reg in a couple of charity matches. All that, though, was a long way in the future and at full-time I couldn't have imagined any of it as we shuffled out of the ground and along Cambridge Street (we always took a slightly different route home), stamping the life back into our frozen feet, everyone around us buzzing at an unexpected Derby victory. Six days later we were back for a Boxing Day game against Portsmouth. Again, Derby won, this time by 3-0, and I began to wonder why everyone was worrying. It was, however, just a blip; by the end of the season the Rams were rock bottom of the table and relegated to play in the Second Division for the first time in almost 30 years. For an eight-year-old boy, though, it was the beginning of a lifelong passion. Derby County became a central part of my life. Then one day, I decided to find out how it all began.

Anton Rippon,
Derby, September 2013

Acknowledgements

A NUMBER of people helped in the production of *Derby County: The Story of a Football Club*. Most significant is Andrew Ward, my co-author on *The Derby County Story* which we first published together in 1984 and which was revised and updated twice, most recently in 1997. Andrew's painstaking research and his words form the basis for parts of the book now in your hands. Without Gerald Mortimer's *Derby County: A Complete Record* tracking down events and players would have been more difficult. Special mention must go to Derby County historian Mike Wilson whose research has decorated the pages of many publications on the Rams over the years. And thanks to all the players – some, alas, no longer with us – who took the time and trouble to talk to me about the football club they loved.

Football in a Higher Order

I T WAS the early autumn of 1884. Queen Victoria was monarch of an empire upon which the sun famously never set, Gladstone was her Prime Minister, and in Derby a man called Francis Ley was celebrating the tenth anniversary of the malleable castings company that he had founded on Osmaston Road. Thanks to its transformation from market town to hotbed of heavy industry, some 85,000 souls lived in Derby, almost triple the number when Victoria ascended the throne 47 years earlier. Most of the newcomers lived in terraced houses in Litchurch, New Normanton, Pear Tree and Rose Hill, areas expanding to accommodate those working long hours in the factories and foundries of the new age. Their jobs were arduous, dirty, often dangerous.

If there was an inclination for leisure, there was little time for it. Certainly, few wandered down to the County Ground on Nottingham Road. If sport was an interest, workers in the heavy industries were unlikely to spend their few free hours watching a cricket team that lost every match. In 1884, Derbyshire CCC couldn't manage even one draw. Off the field, matters were equally desperate. Derbyshire cricket has seldom been anything but cash-strapped. But in the year in which Sophie Tucker was born and John Wisden died, it faced disaster. Could the club continue? The question haunted officials.

The same could not be said for Association Football. Right across Britain, the fledgling sport – goal-nets and penalty-kicks were still years away, even pitch markings weren't as we know them today – was booming. In the FA Cup, now in its 13th season, Derby Midland, drawn from the town's railway works, reached the third round. Another Derbyshire club, Staveley, went further before losing to that year's winners, Blackburn

Rovers. In March 1884 the first-ever Derbyshire Cup Final was staged at the County Ground. Midland and Staveley attracted 7,000 spectators – "the largest attendance ever seen at a football match in Derby". Cricket officials looked on in disbelief and envy. If only their game could attract such numbers …

One keen supporter of the Midland team was William Morley, a young clerk at the railway works. His father, William senior, a member of Derbyshire CCC's committee, lived at the smart end of town, in a large villa near the Arboretum, England's first public park. The younger Morley had already suggested forming a senior football club for the town. Once those eager football supporters overwhelmed the County Ground, Morley senior took no further persuading. A meeting was held at the Bell Hotel in Sadler Gate. The following day, the announcement in the *Derby Daily Telegraph* was simple enough: "The Derbyshire County Cricket Club has decided on the formation of a football club under Association Rules and desires to render football worthy of the patronage blessed upon it by the public by endeavouring to arrange matches with first-class clubs which will enable the public to witness matches in a higher order than have hitherto been played in Derby."

Unsurprisingly, the cricket club wanted to call their football section "Derbyshire County". Equally unsurprisingly, the Derbyshire Football Association, formed a year earlier, ruled that only it could field a team under the county banner. So, Derby County it was. The football team's colours were those of the cricket club – amber, chocolate and pale blue – and the first player was another son of William Morley, Haydn of that ilk, a 23-year-old trainee solicitor who had been playing at full-back for Derby Midland (he was good enough to captain Sheffield Wednesday in the 1890 FA Cup Final). That the second player enlisted – outside-right George Bakewell – was the star of the Derby Midland team signalled the new club's desire to be the best in the district, an ambition that fuelled resentment from other local clubs who began to see their leading players courted by the upstarts at Derby County. When Darley Dale lent the new club their star man, half-back Ernest Hickinbottom (the spelling of whose name caused the local press great difficulty) it was in the naïve belief that it would be simply to give him experience for Darley Dale's greater benefit. They were soon disabused of that notion.

Samuel Richardson, honorary secretary of the football club, assistant secretary of the cricket club and its first-ever captain, would make an early stab at bringing to Derby County the sort of notoriety for which the Rams – as they would eventually become known – would occasionally become infamous. In February 1890, Richardson, then 46, was the target of a stormy annual meeting of the cricket club at which he was accused – by none other than the club's Australian Test star, "Demon" Spofforth – of embezzling funds.

He admitted it. In fact, he had been steadily siphoning off money for 10 years, and not just from the cricket club but from the football club, too. With his wife and several of his six daughters – and £1,000 of the club's money – Richardson fled to Spain, opened a tailor's shop (he'd run a similar business at 40 Babington Lane), obtained the patronage of King Alfonso, and lived to the ripe old age of 93.

But this was all in the future. The football club had yet to play its first match. This was arranged for Saturday, 13 September 1884, at the Woodside ground of Great Lever FC, in the Farnworth district of Bolton. Great Lever had a decent team that included a centre-forward called John Goodall. One day, Derby County and John Goodall would enjoy a much happier relationship than on that early autumn afternoon. Goodall, making his debut in English football, scored five times, Derby conceded six altogether, didn't manage to find the net (of course, there wasn't one anyway) and trooped back to Bolton railway station, their tails well and truly between their legs. It was a shock. This was only a friendly match, but the Derby team wasn't a bad one. The goalkeeper, Borrowash-born Leonard Gillett, was an Oxford Blue who, three years earlier, had helped Old Carthusians win the FA Cup. The forward line contained Benjamin Ward Spilsbury, Findern-born, Repton-educated and a Cambridge Blue who, in less than six months' time, would play for England.

Two weeks later Derby County faced a potentially bigger test: a home friendly against Blackburn Olympic, recent winners of the FA Cup. Around 1,500 people had watched the match at Great Lever. The attendance for Derby County's first home game wasn't recorded, but we do know that men paid a minimum of an old sixpence (the club later reduced that by half) and ladies were admitted free of charge. Entrance was through gates near the Derby Canal bridge on Nottingham Road. The visitors arrived in Derby at 1.08pm and were conveyed from the Midland railway station to the ground by horse-drawn brake.

Within five minutes of the kick-off, Derby County scored their first-ever goal, an honour that fell to the 20-year-old Spilsbury. Olympic drew

Fledgling Rams pass their FA Cup test

THE visit of Aston Villa to the County Ground for a second-round FA Cup-tie in November 1885 was a massive test for the fledgling Derby County. With plenty of Cup experience – they were to win the trophy two years later – Villa fielded two England internationals in Arthur Brown and Howard Vaughton.

In the previous round the Rams had splashed their way to a 3-0 win over Birmingham St George's on a waterlogged County Ground pitch. Now they faced Villa, who had beaten Derby 4-2 in a friendly earlier in the season.

On an overcast day that threatened rain, the extra accommodation that had been erected at the County Ground was well patronised. The pitch was greasy and Derby defended the Nottingham Road goal; Villa had their backs to the Rifle Range end.

In fact, the game should have been played at Perry Barr. Villa had been drawn at home but, for a financial consideration, had agreed to switch the game to Derby in the belief that they would still win easily. How wrong they were.

Evans and Spilsbury both tested Hobson in the Villa goal, and "Jammer" Smith missed a glorious opportunity to put the home side in front. A few minutes later, however, Smith made amends, hammering a shot through the posts. The ball sailed on for over 100 yards before it was retrieved; goal-nets would not be introduced into football until 1891.

Villa came more into the game in the second half, but it was Derby who scored the second goal of the game. Lewis Cooper swung over a left-wing corner, Spilsbury touched it on, and Evans scrambled the ball over the line.

The main threat to the Rams' progress now was the gathering gloom. More than a few cup games had been abandoned with only minutes to play, but fortunately the daylight held and Derby were through, 2-0.

It was a famous victory. At the final whistle, hats and umbrellas were thrown into the air.

One of the heroes had been goalkeeper Walter Luntley. The *Derby Daily Telegraph* commented: "Luntley served his side splendidly between the posts, evincing coolness and judgement. Evans played a dashing game at centre-forward, and Smith and Cooper fairly dogged the Aston backs. Spilsbury was occasionally brilliant, but not constantly so. Of the back divisions, Wharmby, Morley and Williamson worked extremely hard."

In the next round, Derby lost 4-2 to Small Heath Alliance – the club later to become Birmingham City – at Coventry Road. On that occasion Spilsbury was a marked man, Small Heath making sure that he had little room to manoeuvre whenever he received the ball.

Disappointing though that defeat was, Derby's victory over Aston Villa in the previous round had been hugely significant. The Rams would now have no difficulty in arranging a top-class fixture list of friendly matches to boost their coffers.

level but Spilsbury restored Derby's lead. In the second half, Olympic equalised again and then went ahead. Derby scored a third, only for Olympic to go 4-3 in front. It was a thrilling game and it might have ended in a draw. With 10 minutes to play, the splendidly named John Barrington Trapnell Chevalier, a Repton School master and veteran of no less than four FA Cup Finals for Old Etonians, accepted a pass from the more prosaically named "Jammer" Smith and sent in a booming shot that crashed against the Olympic crossbar before rebounding almost halfway down the pitch – quite a feat with that heavy leather ox-bladder football. Nine years earlier, it wouldn't have happened: until 1875 there was no crossbar, just tape. Then an argument would have ensued.

Thus was the measure of the early Derby County: hoary sons of the soil (or, more likely, heavy industry); middle-class clerks; and posh toffs like Chevalier, who, a year later, inherited the family property in Suffolk and established himself as a fruit grower, cider maker and top breeder of Red Poll pedigree cattle. He became a JP and president of the Suffolk Chamber of Agriculture. Alas, there is no record of what happened to "Jammer" Smith.

On the murky day of 8 November 1884, Derby County played their first ever FA Cup match, against Walsall Town.

Paying spectators packed around the County Ground touchline, a handful of privileged officials stood on the steps of the football pavilion (actually the back of the cricket pavilion), and everyone craned their necks for a glimpse of the action. The home side included Derbyshire cricketer Frank Sugg, who was also a fine centre-forward or centre-half (in those days the centre-half was a genuine member of the half-back line, a vital link between attack and defence). Derby won the toss and played with the wind in their favour – and when the wind whipped across the barren Racecourse and through the County Ground, that was a distinct advantage – but fell a goal behind after 20 minutes, were 2-0 down at half-time, and ended up losing 7-0. Sugg, who started the game injured, was virtually a passenger for the entire 90 minutes, and without Spilsbury and Chevalier, Derby had been no match for their more experienced opponents.

Yet by the end of their first season Derby County could look back with some satisfaction. The new club had played 34 matches, of which they had won 14 and drawn nine. It wasn't a bad start.

A Fixity of Fixtures

Football supporters agreed – friendly games lacked the competitive spice that laced cup matches. Aston Villa committeeman William McGregor had the answer: "a fixity of fixtures" with competitive football guaranteed every week. In March 1888 he called a meeting at Anderton's Hotel in London's Fleet Street to discuss the formation of a league. At a subsequent meeting, at the Royal Hotel, Manchester, the following month, the Football League was formed. It has never been called the English League since McGregor always hoped that Scottish clubs would join.

So, on 8 September 1888, 12 clubs from the Midlands and North played the world's first set of league football fixtures. For that historic first day of the Football League those fixtures sent Derby County to Pikes Lane, Bolton. They travelled by train – without the invention of the railway there could never have been a nationwide league – and it was running late, so the match against Bolton Wanderers kicked off half an hour after the scheduled start.

Derby County made the worst possible start to their Football League career. James Kenyon "Kenny" Davenport scored for Wanderers after only two minutes – thus, it is believed, making him scorer of the first-ever Football League goal, despite the late kick-off – and after a quarter of an hour the Rams were 3-0 down. Yet by half-time they had drawn level, and when the referee sounded his whistle for full-time, they were 6-3 winners. Lewis Cooper, Lol Plackett and George Bakewell, all Derbyshire men, had scored their goals "with an ease seldom witnessed". The 5,000-strong crowd booed Bolton off the field. Alas, it was to be Derby's only win in the first half of a season that included seven consecutive defeats and brought about a "meeting of indignation" at the Athenaeum Rooms in Victoria Street where there were calls for the football club to be separated from the "doomed" cricket club. When the season ended with a 3-0 defeat at Blackburn, the Rams – we shall call them that from now on – became one of the four clubs obliged to seek re-election to the new Football League. All survived.

In the summer of 1889 the Rams made two major signings – brothers who could not have been more different. John Goodall was gentle and genial. Although born in London, he spoke with a thick Scottish accent because he had been raised in Ayrshire; his father was a corporal in the Scottish Fusiliers. That the Rams had managed to engage the services of such a high-profile footballer was quite remarkable, so remarkable in fact that on the day he signed, the Derby secretary went around the town pasting up notices announcing the fact. John Goodall was already an England centre-forward. He had been capped while helping Preston win the Football League championship (without losing a game) and lift the FA Cup (without conceding a goal).

As John Goodall was putting his name to a Derby County contract, his brother, Archie, was trying his best to get out of having done the same. Thanks to the peripatetic nature of their father's profession, Archie Goodall was born in Belfast and would one day play his international football for Ireland, once the Irish FA had lifted its ban on non-resident players representing the Emerald Isle. He was a rumbustuous character. A Derby solicitor had arranged for the Goodalls to sign for the Rams, but while John quickly scotched the rumour that he would pull out of the agreement, Archie said that he had changed his mind. Although he had started 1888-89 with Preston, Archie had moved to Aston Villa – the first-ever Football League transfer to take place during a season – and now he wanted to remain with Villa. Only when he was told that if he reneged then he would be banned altogether for two seasons did he reluctantly change his mind.

Derby County were to have their hands full with Archie Goodall. He was up before the magistrates for punching a spectator who had barracked him. On one occasion he walked off the pitch after 90 minutes of an end-of-season United Counties League championship decider against West Brom. Extra-time was to be played but Archie claimed that his season's contract had ended. If Derby wanted him for another 30 minutes then they would have to pay him extra. They refused and carried on with 10 men. He also left them with 10 men for a league game at Preston, at the last minute refusing to travel because his wife was ill. When he wasn't playing football, Archie busied himself in the backyard of his house in Wolfa Street, building a large iron hoop. That summer he toured Europe and America with a strongman act, part of which involved him "walking" around the hoop. Once he made the 650-mile round trip from Derby to Kilmarnock riding a bay cob, completing the entire journey there and back in five days. What would be the commercial value of such a character today?

On 19 March 1892, the Rams couldn't have the County Ground because of a race meeting. Step forward Francis Ley, the man we met at the beginning of this story. He allowed the use of his works sports ground in the Pear Tree district of the town. The players had mixed feelings: the turf was much better at the County Ground, where the replay of the 1886 FA Cup Final had been staged, but the facilities at Ley's 12-acre sports ground were better. The Leys' ground was quite a complex – football, cricket and other sports were played there – but it was one corner that staged the Rams' game against Sunderland. On a business trip to the USA, Ley had been fascinated by the game of baseball. On his return to Derby he set about constructing a baseball diamond and outfield on his sports ground. It was here that Derby County's first home game away from the County Ground took place. Football at a baseball ground – surely not?

The Twisting Tormentor

On 3 September 1892, the Rams met Stoke – they didn't add "City" for another 33 years – at the Victoria Ground. And William Parker, Derby County's first paid secretary, had a red face, a very red face. The 39-year-old accountant had offices at 4 Amen Alley, a quaint little street in the shadow of All Saints' Church that, in 1927, would become Derby Cathedral. The house itself is long gone, cars now parked where once Parker pored over the early balance sheets of Derby County. In 1892, it was more a case of William Parker picking his way through horse droppings. And on this September day he was really was in a mess. He had been a day late in registering three of Derby's professional players, Ernest Hickinbottom, outside-right Sam Mills and inside-forward Jimmy McLachlan. Into their places stepped Harry Garden, Fred Ekins, and an 18-year-old called Stephen Bloomer. More than 1,000 travelling Derby fans wondered who the pale, young lad was. So did the local Stoke newspaper reporter. The only journalist covering the match, he recognised hardly any of the visiting players, and when he telegraphed back his report that Derby County had won 3-1, he credited two of their goals to Johnny McMillan. But it was the new boy, Steve Bloomer, who had scored them.

The debutant had been understandably nervous. But when no less a star than John Goodall urged: "Go on yourself, lad, and shoot," well, what else could he do? The *Derby Daily Telegraph* commented: "Young Bloomer ought to be heard of again in the first team and if he continues to improve as he has done hitherto, then he will make one of the finest forwards in Association Football." Quite how the writer knew that if he hadn't been at the game, I don't know. Presumably he had spoken to one or more of Bloomer's teammates, or maybe he had seen the youngster before. Whatever, more prophetic words have surely never been written about a young footballer. Bloomer's goals had come three minutes into the start of each half. They would be the first of 332 that he would score for Derby County. No player in the club's history has ever got near that number. And no player ever will.

In one game for Derby Swifts, Bloomer scored 14 goals. In March 1891, just after his 17th birthday, Derby Midland signed him on. Later that year Midland folded and the Rams absorbed the railway club and all its assets as Derby County and Derbyshire CCC finally went their separate ways. One such asset, almost certainly the most valuable, was Steve Bloomer. He joined Derby County as an amateur in June that year, and in his first game scored four times against Darley Dale. The following April he signed professional forms – 7s 6d (38p) per week. "I signed up for that figure meek as a lamb," he wrote years later. The lamb was to grow into arguably the greatest ever Ram.

On 21 January 1893, Bloomer made his first appearance in the FA Cup. Nearly 3,000 of the 20,000 crowd at Olive Grove, Sheffield, had travelled from Derby. John Goodall scored first against The Wednesday, then Bloomer made it 2-0. But the home team fought back, the game went into extra-time and The Wednesday found the winner. The Rams heard that one of the home players had not been properly registered. They protested, and a rematch was set for the County Ground nine days later. John Goodall scored the only goal of that game but then The Wednesday protested that Bloomer had signed professional forms for another club before joining the Rams. The young lad had fought off all representations from Burton United before unwittingly putting his signature to a signing-on form when he thought he was merely giving his autograph. The FA accepted that he had been tricked but still ordered a third match to be played, back at Olive Grove. This time the result stood: The Wednesday 4, Derby County 2.

Steve Bloomer's first season saw the Rams finish 13th – there were 16 clubs in what was now the First Division – and his goal against the eventual champions, Sunderland's "Team, of all Talents", earned an unexpected home point and helped towards avoiding relegation. But he was already becoming a marked young man. In October 1893, a match against Newton Heath (the club that would become Manchester United) at the County

Ground erupted into violence, and Bloomer was the main target. The Heathens' left-back John Clements, a former Notts County player, put through his own goal, and Johnny McMillan made it 2-0. Newton Heath disputed the goal and threatened to walk off. Then the visitors' defence set to. The referee's report sums it up: "Clements was cautioned several times for foully playing Bloomer, while Donaldson deliberately stabbed Leiper in the groin and thigh. Perrins deliberately kicked Archie Goodall without the slightest provocation." The Rams won 2-0. Quite how Archie Goodall reacted to being kicked is not recorded.

On 1 September 1894, Derby arrived at champions Sunderland for their first match of the season, only to learn that the appointed referee, Fred Kirkham of Preston, had missed his train. The match started with a deputy official, John Conqueror, in charge. At half-time Sunderland were winning 3-0 when Mr Kirkham arrived, out of breath and a little embarrassed. The Rams were offered the choice of restarting the game from scratch, which, not surprisingly, they elected to do. But the next first half also ended with the home side 3-0 ahead, and after playing a third "half" with a gale in their faces, Derby conceded five more goals, making it 11 on the afternoon, only eight of which counted, of course.

Whatever the ludicrous circumstances, an 8-0 opening day defeat could not be ignored. By the end of the season the Rams were forced to play a "Test Match" – a 19th-century version of the play-offs, only for bottom clubs – against Notts County. It was staged at Walnut Street (later Filbert Street; they do like their nuts in Leicester) where, five minutes from the end, the Rams were trailing 1-0 and John Goodall was limping heavily in those days when substitutes had never been considered. Goodall rallied his men: "Now then boys, there'll be no Second Division football for us!" He was correct. Jimmy Methven hammered in a free-kick from 30 yards out, the ball cannoned off the back of a Notts player who had taken evasive action, and Bloomer whacked the rebound into the net. Now it was exciting. So exciting that the daughter of a Derby director fainted and another Rams official squeezed his pocket watch so tightly that he broke it. The Rams forced three corners, one after the other. From the third, taken by John Goodall, McMillan scored the winning goal. Back in the dressing room the Derby players were ecstatic, although there were probably no high-fives. Only Archie Goodall looked unhappy: "We should have had a dollytubful," he moaned.

So it was First Division football again in 1895-96. Before the season began, Derby County became a limited liability company. And now they could use initial capital letters when referring to the Baseball Ground that was purchased from Francis Ley to become the permanent – well, for 102 years anyway – home of the Rams. The industrialist was a great benefactor. He spent £7,000 to increase the capacity of the Rams' new home from 4,000 to 20,000, and it was half-full when Sunderland were the visitors on the opening day of the season. Bloomer scored twice and Derby won 2-0. It was a great start and it got better and better. By the end of the season the Rams were runners up to Aston Villa.

It was an FA Cup tie against Villa that had seen the Baseball Ground's capacity increased even further. The potential for a big crowd was so great that the Derby directors ordered a new stand – to be known as the Railway Stand – to be built. The attendance that day is recorded as 20,000 but it was probably more. The new stand was only half-finished and workmen had to make it secure during the game. It would take the capacity to 27,000. There was a mighty roar when the Rams ran out "as fit as fiddles and as lively as kittens" after their "special Cup training" at Ashover. Soon they were 4-0 in front – Bloomer, inevitably, had scored twice – and although Villa pulled back two goals, it was the Rams who went into the hat for the next round. In fact, they went all the way to the semi-finals before losing 2-1 to Wolves at Perry Barr.

In 1896-97 the Rams finished third, and there was another appearance in the FA Cup semi-final, this time against Everton at the Victoria Ground. Both Goodalls scored but it was the Merseysiders who went into the Final with a 3-2 victory. First Division runners-up and then third place, and consecutive FA Cup semi-finals – Derby County were becoming a football power.

Third Time Unlucky

On Saturday, 16 April 1898, thousands of football supporters from the East Midlands boarded trains for London. From Derby and from Nottingham they flooded, each paying 4s (20p) for a workman's return. Their destination was the Crystal Palace at Sydenham where they would be part of a 60,826 crowd at the FA Cup Final between the Rams and Nottingham Forest. Derby's players could look back on an Easter Monday hammering of Forest at the Baseball Ground in which Bloomer scored a hat-trick. That afternoon the Rams hit five altogether, and Forest managed no goals at all. But several of the visitors' Cup Final line-up were watching from the stand.

As kick-off time approached at the Crystal Palace, the Rams couldn't find Archie Goodall. Steve Bloomer takes up the story: "In those days Cup Final tickets could be bought in any numbers, and Archie Goodall had speculated in them. On the day of the Final, he had a lot of tickets left on his hands. Of course, he did not wish to lose on the transaction and so, when the crowd was rolling up to the Crystal Palace, he went outside the grandstand to try to sell his tickets. We players knew where Archie had gone, but the trouble began when we were all stripped and waiting in the passage outside the room, ready to go on to the field, with no Archie Goodall." The start was delayed until Archie reappeared.

After 19 minutes, Arthur Capes put Forest ahead. Twelve minutes later Bloomer equalised with a header from Leiper's free-kick – the ball bouncing off the underside of the crossbar and over the line – but Capes restored the Forest lead. In the second half Bloomer shot wide when he had only the goalkeeper to beat, and then John Goodall's shot hit the bar. With four minutes remaining, Johnny McPherson scored a third for Forest, and Lord Rosebery presented the FA Cup to the wrong side of the River Trent. Derby County supporters trudged mournfully back to the railway station.

Twelve months later, the Rams were back at the Crystal Palace. Their league season had already been a remarkable one. On a bog of a Baseball Ground pitch the Rams beat Sheffield Wednesday 9-0 (Bloomer scored six) and the following week hammered Wolves 6-2. There was a 7-1 defeat at Aston Villa, and a 5-5 draw with Everton at the Baseball Ground where Derby had trailed 5-2 with only 15 minutes to go.

Before the semi-final, the Derby directors – like most clubs the Rams still had no manager – decided to take the players to Buxton for more "special cup training" – one is tempted to ask why, if it was so special, they did not do it every week – but Archie Goodall refused to travel, claiming that "private business" rendered it necessary for him to remain in Derby. The club suspended him for "inattention to training". Against Stoke at Molineux, Archie was sorely missed and midway through the first half the Potters took the lead. Then Bloomer scored a goal of brilliant invention, back-heading a high bouncing ball as the goalkeeper rushed out to collect it. In the second half it was all Bloomer. He scored twice more to complete yet another hat-trick, and the Rams were back in the FA

Cup Final, this time facing Sheffield United who, in the other semi-final, had beaten Liverpool 1-0 at the Baseball Ground.

John Goodall, now in the veteran stage, travelled as a reserve, thus missing out on a fourth FA Cup Final. And, of course, there was no Archie, who was still in disgrace. The Rams were favourites – despite being reigning Football League champions, Sheffield United were now fourth from bottom of the First Division – and at half-time they led 1-0, through a goal from Boag. Moments into the second half, Bloomer saw his shot hit a post, and then another effort from the great Steve was blocked by the massive frame of "Fatty" Foulke, United's 21-stone goalkeeper. Then came the turning point of the game. Wing-half Johnny May (later to join Rangers and captain Scotland) was injured. Down to 10 men, the Rams brought forward Willie MacDonald back to take May's place but MacDonald was no defensive player. Fourteen minutes into the second half, the Blades' captain Ernest "Nudger" Needham (who later played cricket for Derbyshire) curled over a centre from which "Cocky" Bennett levelled the scores. Bloomer wrote later: "After the subsequent reorganisation weakened our left flank, Needham recognised our plight and directed his whole attack down there … " Now it was one-way traffic and the tastily named Beers and Almond made it 3-1 before Fred Priest added a fourth against desperately demoralised Derby.

Could the Rams make it a hat-trick of FA Cup Finals? Not immediately. The following season they went out in the first round, losing a replay 3-0 at Sunderland. The year after that Bolton knocked them out, 1-0. In the First Division in those seasons, Derby finished sixth and 12th respectively. John Goodall moved to New Brighton in the summer of 1899. Archie Goodall was still moaning, still upset about being left out of the Cup Final team, and missed the first four matches of 1899-1900 after initially refusing to re-sign. His life could have been much worse. On 7 November 1899, as the Rams set off for a First Division match at Blackburn, some of their supporters were setting off in another direction, marching from Normanton Barracks to the Midland station. They were Sherwood Foresters reservists, called up to fight in the Boer War. Over the next two days, hundreds more followed. Some would not see home again.

Steve Bloomer was also in a rare warlike mood, sent off after kicking out at Bert Sharp of Everton after being on the receiving end of some brutal tackles. Bloomer was affronted at his dismissal and submitted

Cup-tie that sent the factories quiet

WHEN Derby County entertained Portsmouth on a Wednesday afternoon in late February 1902, interest was so great that local factory owners bowed to inevitable mass absenteeism and simply closed down. The Rams' FA Cup quarter-final replay against Pompey was the talk of the town. Companies including the Midland Railway works and Handyside's foundry shut their gates at noon. And after a quick pint and a sandwich, most of their workers were hurrying to the Baseball Ground for the 2pm kick-off.

The replay was the Rams' first home game since 11 January, and despite the midweek afternoon kick-off, it attracted Derby's biggest home attendance of the season after the Boxing Day clash with Newcastle United.

The crowd of 17,836 included players from Aston Villa, Nottingham Forest and West Bromwich Albion, all of who had rushed to the Baseball Ground after training. There were few Portsmouth supporters present, though. No special trains or charabancs had been organised from the naval town.

Within eight minutes, the Rams were two goals in front. First there was what the *Derby Daily Telegraph* reporter described as "a scrimmage", from which Steve Bloomer extracted the ball and fed Warren, who hammered his shot past Irish international goalkeeper, Matt Reilly.

Then Scottish centre-forward John Boag exchanged passes with Dick Wombwell, a utility forward who had been signed from Ilkeston Town. Boag took the return ball and extended the Rams' lead. After 15 minutes, Warren added a third goal for Derby, the ball slipping through Reilly's hands.

Pompey battled back to score through former Villa and England player, Steve Smith, who pounced on a loose ball to beat the gangling Jack Fryer in Derby's goal. The Rams goalkeeper, "with the sun shining brilliantly in his eyes", then saved well from Corrin and MacAuley, and also did well to stop an effort from England's Daniel Cunliffe.

The Rams resumed in the same mood. After 55 minutes Bloomer, "who had just had one of his hot cannons", beat Reilly with a left-foot shot. Then Archie Goodall let the ball run to Bloomer, who scored Derby's fifth goal to put the result apparently beyond doubt.

But there was to be a nail-biting finish. Jimmy Methven upended Smith, and Edgar Chadwick, yet another England player, scored from the penalty spot. When Cunliffe hit an unstoppable shot past Fryer, it was 5-3 but Pompey's hopes of a sensational fightback disappeared when Bloomer completed his hat-trick three minutes from time.

The semi-final, against Sheffield United, took three games to settle. Warren put the Rams in front in the first game, at The Hawthorns, before United equalised with Rams goalkeeper Fryer "more interested in appealing for offside than in stopping the ball". Wombwell got the Rams' goal in another 1-1 draw, this time at Molineux. At the City Ground, Fred Priest administered the last rites to Derby County.

four sheets of handwritten "evidence" to support his appeal. He was still suspended for a fortnight.

Derby County now had their first manager in the way that we would recognise the post today. In 1900 they appointed 39-year-old Harry Newbould, who already served as club secretary, to take charge of playing affairs. In his youth Newbould, an accountant by profession, had played outside-right for Derby St Luke's and had also been a notable sprinter. When the Rams became a limited liability company in 1896, he was taken on as assistant secretary to W. D. "Billy" Clark. Clark also enjoyed the title of "manager" and, indeed, long-serving full back Jimmy Methven later referred to him as "Wily Willie" because of his unorthodox way of attracting players to Derby. Newbould, though, was the first "hands-on" manager.

Until late March 1903, the Rams were contenders for the Football League championship. Then they lost 1-0 at home to Everton, a result that heralded a slide which saw Derby win only one more game – and draw only one more – to finish ninth. Towards the end of that run they had another engagement – against Bury in the FA Cup Final. The Rams had reached the Crystal Palace for the third time in five years but had picked up injuries along the way, not least to Bloomer who was suffering from an ankle so swollen it was a week before he could pull on a football boot. Against Millwall in the semi-final, winger George Davis, who would play for England the following season, was concussed after tripping on matting put down for the comfort of the linesmen. And on Easter Monday, goalkeeper Jack "String" Fryer pulled a groin muscle while stretching for a cross at Middlesbrough. At Ayresome Park the Rams finished with nine men, with Welsh international full-back Charlie Morris in goal and half-back Charlie Leckie also in the dressing room.

It was an unhappy Derby contingent that travelled by train to London on the Friday afternoon of 17 April 1903. The following morning, thousands of supporters followed them. At St Pancras station those supporters found three rooms set aside for them with 400 barrels of beer, 200 crates of bottled beer and a plentiful supply of spirits with which to slake their thirsts. Meanwhile, an eve-of-match trip to the theatre had failed to raise the spirits of the Derby team. When they returned to their hotel, goalkeeper Fryer was in obvious discomfort. That night he got little sleep, still troubled by the pain in his groin. Reserve goalkeeper Frank Davies, from Birkenhead, had yet to make a senior appearance for the

Rams but manager Harry Newbould and the directors were prepared to let him make his debut in a Cup Final. Davies even offered to let Fryer have his medal, win or lose, but the tall goalkeeper refused to give up his place. On the other hand Bloomer, worried that he might let down teammates and supporters alike, declared himself unfit.

By half-time, things had gone better than anyone in the Derby camp had dared hope. True, Bury led 1-0. But that wasn't an insurmountable deficit. The goal, though, had come because Fryer was incapacitated. Fully fit, he would probably have stopped the bouncing ball. As it was, 20 minutes into the first half a lofted effort from George Ross looped clean over Fryer's head and into the net. Bury, fielding six of the team that had won the FA Cup three years earlier, began the second half in complete control. Charlie Sager put Bury further ahead, and in trying to prevent the goal Fryer took another knock and had to leave the field. Morris went in goal again, only to see Joe Leeming chip the ball past him: 3-0. Fryer returned but within a minute Willie Wood made it 4-0. Then Jack Plant scored number five. Morris took over again, but neither he nor a fit Fryer would have stopped Bury's sixth goal from Leeming. Bury hit the woodwork twice more, and the game descended into near farce when Methven went in goal to give Morris a breather, and should have conceded a penalty after handling the ball before he had informed the referee of the change. The official, Jack Adams of Birmingham, must have felt sorry for desperate Derby and he waved play on to complete the most one-sided Final in FA Cup history. A few days later, the brilliant but troublesome Archie Goodall left for Plymouth Argyle.

Ups and Downs

FOR DERBY COUNTY supporters the 10 years leading to the First World War would bring a range of emotions: relegation, promotion, relegation once more, then another promotion, together with the loss and subsequent return to a hero's welcome of their star player. The period started with the Rams' seventh FA Cup semi-final in nine years. Clubs in any era would be pleased with that. However, there was to be no fourth trip to the Crystal Palace. Bolton won 1-0 at Molineux, leaving the Rams to concentrate on avoiding relegation, which they did by only two points.

In welcome contrast, the beginning of 1904-05 brought 14 points from the first 11 games – only two points for a win – but it couldn't last. Championship hopes were soon put to bed and the Rams finished 11th. Only England men Bloomer and Davis, and George Richards looked settled before the latter pair missed chunks of the season through injury. It had been a disappointing campaign, but the Rams winning their first five games of 1905-06 brought high hopes for supporters.

They were hopes to be dashed in the most emphatic manner. The perfect start soon became an imperfect progress and the Rams dropped down the table. Then, on Friday, 16 March 1906, the day before the Rams were due to play Woolwich Arsenal at Plumstead, news broke in Derby that the previous evening the club had transferred Steve Bloomer to Middlesbrough. What a thing to do – sell the player who had been your leading scorer for each of the past 13 seasons, and had already scored 12 goals in 23 games that season. And not only that – sell him to fellow relegation strugglers. Rams fans were furious. Middlesbrough had tried to sign Steve the previous season, and when rebuffed instead paid a world record transfer fee of £1,000 to Sunderland for their England centre-forward, Alf Common. Boro were denounced for "buying" their way out of relegation and the Football League introduced a transfer fee limit. Under the new regulation the Rams received £750 for Bloomer – more than the new ceiling – because they included a reserve-team defender called Emor "Jack" Ratcliff.

Harry Newbould was against selling Bloomer, but the Derby board insisted. Losing the club's leading scorer made the struggle to avoid relegation even more difficult, and although six points from seven matches in April saw Derby to safety by four points – Middlesbrough also stayed up with a better goal-average than relegated Forest – it did not conceal huge weaknesses. In the final four games of the season the Rams suffered two heavy defeats, 6-0 at Aston Villa, and, even more alarming, 7-0 at Wolves, a team that was about to finish bottom of the table. Newbould, looked to his future. In July he took over at Manchester City.

On 7 August 1906, the Rams announced Newbould's replacement – 38-year-old Jimmy Methven, who had just completed 15 years as a solid defender for the club and was veteran of its three FA Cup Finals. That season Methven would make three appearances as a player-manager, taking his final total of Rams senior games to 511. He was the first Rams manager whose role wasn't complicated by also being the club's secretary. He could concentrate solely on playing matters, although the directors still had the final say.

Methven's first game in charge was at Bramall Lane on 1 September 1906. Sheffield United won 2-0, and that set the scene for another season of struggle. By the penultimate home game of the season, there was still a slim hope of survival, especially when Everton were beaten 5-2 at the Baseball Ground. The next game was also at home, to Bristol City, which then left a visit to Woolwich Arsenal on the final day of the season. Bristol were leading 2-1 when the Rams were thrown a lifeline: Freddie Wheatcroft, who'd played for England as an amateur, was bowled over in the penalty area. Ben Hall, usually a reliable taker of spot-kicks, stepped up – and missed. In the second half City scored again and the Rams' trip to Plumstead was academic. They faced Second Division football for the first time, and a £632 loss on the year prompted chairman W. T. Morley to ask a public meeting: "Is the club worth continuing or not?" It was agreed that it was, and new shares were issued.

For most of their first season in the Second Division, the Rams sat on top of the table, thanks in no small part to the goals of Alf "Snobby" Bentley, who Methven had signed from Alfreton Town in December 1906. On 14 September 1907, in the third match of the season, he scored all the goals in a 4-0 win at Barnsley. When the season ended he had 27 in 35 league matches, breaking Bloomer's 1900-01 record of 24 in 27 games. But, thanks to them losing their last five games, Derby could finish only sixth.

Ben Warren, a current England international, had remained loyal to Derby in a bid to help them recover their status, but at the end of the season he returned to the First Division by signing for Chelsea. Warren enjoyed his football at Stamford Bridge, but not his time in London. Desperately homesick, each Saturday night he caught the first available train back to his South Derbyshire home. Despite his status as an England regular, he cut a sad figure and met a sad end. Certified insane, he was committed to Derbyshire Lunatic Asylum and died in November 1917, aged only 38.

In 1908-09 another absorbing FA Cup run compromised the Rams' battle for promotion. Derby reached their eighth semi-final where they met First Division Bristol City at Stamford Bridge. With only seconds remaining, the Rams were leading 1-0 through a Ted Garry goal when Jack Nicholas – father of the man who was to lift the FA Cup for Derby in 1946 – inexplicably handled in the penalty area. Derbyshire-born Willis Rippon drove home the spot-kick and the teams moved to St Andrew's for the replay. There, two minutes from half-time of a fairly even game, Nicholas was ruled to have handled again – this time the general opinion was that he had been ill-served – and again Rippon scored from the spot. Davis equalised just after half-time, but this was going to be Bristol's day. Robert Hardy soon restored their lead and it was they who went on to meet Manchester United in the 1909 FA Cup Final. The Cup run had been exciting but it probably cost the Rams promotion. They finished fifth, nine points adrift of going back up.

Derby County had a new-look team. Apart from Bentley, the man with a happy knack of scoring goals, they included a full-back from Newhall Swifts, Jack Aitkin who would go on to make 308 senior appearance for Derby. Jimmy Bagshaw, a wing-half from Graham Street Prims, was also establishing himself; he would make 240 appearances for the Rams. And there was Tommy Barbour, a wing-half or full-back from Scottish junior football; he would play 294 times. Horace Barnes had made a great impression after signing from Wadsley Bridge, a Sheffield junior club, and his contribution to Derby County's cause would ultimately be 78 goals from 167 games. In May 1909, another Scot, inside-forward Jimmy Beauchop, was transferred from Crystal Palace to Derby, for whom he would make 135 appearances and score 72 goals.

Once again in the Second Division, Derby County flattered to deceive, and they also had to endure bad publicity when drunken Rams fans ran though the streets of Birmingham following an FA Cup defeat at Villa Park. An outraged Colonel Ludlow wrote to a local newspaper, describing Derby supporters as "utterly undisciplined".

The same could not always be said of the team. On the final day of the 1909-10 season, if other results went their way then Derby County needed to beat West Brom at The Hawthorns in order to regain their First Division place. Albion were in mid-table with no chance of promotion and in no danger of relegation. But the Rams were without goalkeeper Ernald Scattergood – another Derbyshire-born custodian, from Ripley Athletic – and also missing first-choice wingers, Davie Donald and Billy Grimes. Horace Bailey, a 38-year-old former Leicester Fosse and England goalkeeper and 1908 Olympic gold football medal winner, stood in for Scattergood. Bailey, who in September 1899 had helped the Rams Reserves when he was working as a clerk at the Midland Railway, had once let in 12 goals against Nottingham Forest the day after the Fosse players had celebrated rather too liberally at a teammate's wedding reception. On this day at The Hawthorns he was injured after only eight minutes, leaving Derby with 10 men and George Richards between the posts. Bailey returned, hobbling, was twice knocked out, doused with cold water from the trainer's bucket, and gallantly held on. At the other end the Rams forwards let him down. The nearest they came to scoring was in the dying seconds when Beauchop's header from a corner scraped the bar on its way for a goal-kick. The match ended goalless. Manchester City and Oldham Athletic were promoted. Derby County were in danger of becoming stuck in the Second Division.

See The Conquering Hero Come

Sixth, fifth and fourth, it seemed that Derby County just could not make that final leap back into the First Division. Manager Jimmy Methven had a plan, though. In late September 1910 he asked Steve Bloomer to meet him at Middlesbrough railway station. Bloomer had recommended to Methven that he should sign the Boro half-back, Tommy Wilson, and so was under the impression that the Rams manager was travelling north to set up that transfer. But Methven had a different purpose. "How would you like to come back to Derby?" he asked. Neither Bloomer nor his wife had settled in the North-East. Methven told him: "Derby, with all its slow motions, is worth coming back to." Steve could give only one answer. And so there was a special buzz in the streets of Derby on the first Saturday of October 1910, as Rams fans hurried to the Baseball Ground for what should have been a routine Second Division game against Lincoln City. This was no ordinary game, however. A Derby County legend was coming home.

"No more sensational news as this could have been anticipated by any supporter of the Rams," declared the *Derbyshire Football Express* – and when Steve Bloomer arrived at the Midland Station, hundreds turned up to catch a glimpse of him on his way to his new home in Portland Street, a few hundred yards from the Baseball Ground. In his time at Ayresome Park, Bloomer had scored 62 goals in 130 League and Cup games and added two England caps to his tally.

"The transfer fee we paid for Steve was £100 and that sum was nearly the entrance gate at the very first match," Methven recalled. The Rams had made a poor start to the 1910-11 season. Losing 4-1 at home to Chelsea on the opening day, they won only one of their first five games. For their sixth game, however, things were different, gloriously different. When Steve Bloomer led out Derby County on that sunny October afternoon, he was greeted by a brass band playing *See The Conquering Hero Come*, and by the cheers of 12,000 spectators, double the attendance for the previous home game, against Blackpool. "The welcome I received from the Derby crowd brought tears to my eyes," he said.

The Rams kicked off towards the Osmaston end and, after 20 minutes, the old maestro struck, tucking the ball away after Lincoln goalkeeper Tommy Fern had become tangled up with Derby's Davie Donald and Horace Barnes. Despite Fern having to leave the field with a strained side, thus reducing Lincoln to 10 men and no proper goalkeeper, the score was still 1-0 at the interval, after which Fern resumed his position. Ten minutes after the break, however, Barnes headed home a Donald corner, and after 65 minutes it was 3-0 when Bloomer scored his second from a penalty. With 15 minutes remaining, Fern gave up his brave attempt and was helped off again, looking back over his shoulder just in time to see Beauchop head Derby's fourth. In the last minute, Beauchop made it 5-0 and Steve Bloomer's homecoming was complete.

At the end of the season, the Rams stood sixth and Bloomer was top scorer with 20 goals from 28 games. With Steve back in the team, there was real belief that at last the Rams could return to the top flight, and although the 1911-12 season began with a 3-0 defeat at Clapton Orient, a three-month unbeaten run that included six consecutive victories produced 25 points from a possible 28. By January, the Rams looked to be storming to the Second Division title, but then a 4-0 defeat at Stockport on New Year's Day was the first of six games without a win. This time, however, it was only a blip. In the last 11 matches of the season, Derby conceded only one goal. Their final game was against Barnsley who were beaten 2-0 at Oakwell where only 4,000 bothered to turn up to see that season's FA Cup Finalists. When the Rams got back to Derby Midland station, they found 20,000 fans waiting to greet the Second Division champions.

The Rams went up with 54 points, the same as runners-up Chelsea but with a better goal-average. Goals had again come from Bloomer (18) and Beauchop (16), but Harry Leonard, signed from Middlesbrough in October that season to replace Bentley who had moved to Bolton Wanderers at the end of the previous campaign, contributed 17 goals. Perhaps the biggest change, though, had come in defence where centre-half Frank Buckley (from Birmingham) and left-back Charlie Betts (from Newcastle United) were early-season signings who made a huge difference.

Back in the First Division for 1912-13, the Rams did well enough, finishing seventh, thanks in part to an unbeaten run in April that saw them win three and draw two of the last five matches of the season. In January, Bauchop had scored a hat-trick in a 5-0 win over Spurs at the Baseball Ground. Four months later he was a Tottenham player. Despite that encouraging season, and its especially encouraging finale, there was gloom on the horizon. In 1913-14, after only one year in the top flight, the Rams were relegated again. Bloomer, now 40, played only five times, while Leonard missed one-third of the games because of injury. In October the Rams paid £1,500 to Glossop for inside-forward Jimmy Moore but, although Moore scored 10 goals in his 27 games, it wasn't enough to make a difference.

It was obvious that Horace Barnes was too good to play in the Second Division. At the end of the season he moved to Manchester City who were happy to equal the British record transfer fee of £2,500. Yet, even without his goals, the Rams went straight back to the First Division, and as champions again. The only person who might have spoiled things was Kaiser Wilhelm II. In early August 1914 the German army poured over the Belgian frontier to spring the trigger that started the First World War. The Football League and the FA Cup was allowed to continue but everyone connected with the game was denounced as both unpatriotic and unproductive. In November 1914, *The Times* carried a letter from the historian A. H. Pollard: " ... Every club that employs a professional football player is bribing a much-needed recruit away from enlistment and every spectator who pays his gate money is contributing so much towards a German victory." The FA responded by claiming that 500,000 recruits had already been raised by football organisations, that of 5,000 professionals, some 2,000 were already in the services, and only 600 unmarried professional footballers had failed to heed the call.

While all this was going on Steve Bloomer was interned – with spectacularly bad timing, in July 1914 he'd gone off to coach Berlin Britannia – and Derby County were making their way back to the First Division. On the first day of the season the Rams trounced Barnsley 7-0 at the Baseball Ground with Norman Fordham, signed from non-League Ashford the previous February, scoring a hat-trick. That war had been declared a month earlier was probably the reason why there were barely 2,000 present to see the Rams win, but as the season progressed so attendances grew and when Derby entertained promotion rivals Preston for the final game on 24 April, there were 12,000 in the ground. The result put the Rams three points ahead of Preston who went up with them. Moore ended the season with 22 goals. Leonard, recovered from injury, finished with 19, while Tom Benfield, who'd joined from Leicester Fosse in June 1914, scored 15.

The Rams would now have to wait four years to resume their place in the First Division, but Benfield would not live to see it. He'd left the Leicestershire Regiment to sign for Fosse and now he rejoined it. On 19 September 1918, Sergeant Tommy Benfield died of wounds after being shot by a sniper on the Western Front. Three other players to have worn the Rams shirt died during the "war to end all wars". Wing-half George Brooks who, like Benfield, had played in the 1914-15 promotion season, was killed in November 1918 while serving with the 2nd/4th Battalion, Yorkshire and Lancashire Regiment. Reg Callender, a Cambridge Blue and England amateur international who had played five times in 1913-14, died in October 1915 from injuries sustained in an accident with a hand grenade while he was serving with the Durham Light Infantry in France. And in October 1918, Bernard Vann, who'd played three times in 1906-07, was shot through the heart by a sniper's bullet and died instantly. Vann, who was serving in the Sherwood Foresters, was awarded a posthumous VC for his valour in an earlier action.

In May 1915 the Football League suspended the competition, and after the "Khaki Cup Final" of April that year, when thousands of uniformed soldiers were in a 50,000 crowd at Old Trafford to see Sheffield United beat Chelsea 3-0, the FA Cup was also put into storage. The Rams carried on for 1915-16 in the newly formed Midland Section of the war league but they fared badly and took no further part. When the war ended in November 1918 it was too late to start a proper football season. In March and April 1919, the Rams played in the four-team Victory Shield competition and, for what it was worth, finished joint top with Wolves and West Brom. Then they began to look forward to First Division football once more.

However, on 17 February 1919 the mayor of Derby, Alderman William Blews Robotham, chaired a public meeting at the Guildhall "to save Derby County FC from the very real threat of extinction". The club owed its bank £1,300 and, according to Rams director Bendle Moore, the board would not carry on unless public money was raised, otherwise Derby County would have to "sell their players to meet their liabilities and the pass out". Thanks to a subscription fund, the forming of a Working Men's Committee designed to encourage workers to buy shares, and the remarkable benevolence of Sir Gordon Ley who became president and agreed to forego rent owed on the Baseball Ground, the club survived and the Rams could take their place in the First Division after all.

Ninety Minutes From Wembley

After five matches of 1919-20, unbeaten Derby County topped the First Division. With five matches remaining the Rams were relegation candidates. On 5 April 1920, Everton arrived at the Baseball Ground in confident mood. Although themselves in the bottom half of the table, three days earlier they had beaten Derby 4-0 at Goodison. Deep into the return fixture that the Rams desperately needed to win, the score stood at 1-1 when Alf Quantrill, an outside-left signed from Lincolnshire junior football at the start of the war, swung over a corner and who should come racing into the penalty to head the winner? Why, Jack Aitkin. In 13 years with the Rams it was his first goal. Derby won three of their last four games, including a 5-0 thrashing of third-placed Chelsea, and drew the other to avoid relegation by two points.

The forwards had struggled to take their chances – many provided by George Thornewell, a tiny winger who had played wartime football for Rolls-Royce – and goalscoring also proved a major problem as the new season unfolded. In their first 19 matches, the Rams netted only 11 times. It wasn't surprising that the first victory didn't arrive until their ninth match, when Manchester City lost 3-0 at the Baseball Ground. One of the goals that day came from an Egyptian, Tewfik Abdallah, who had been spotted by Rams player Tommy Barbour when Barbour played for an army team against Cairo's International Sporting Club. Tewfik soon became known as "Toothpick" and in his short time at Derby proved popular with players and supporters alike. But, as interesting a signing as he was, Abdallah certainly wasn't going to be the answer. In January 1921, Derby decided to spend some money on their goalscoring problem. They paid £3,000 to Cowdenbeath, for centre-forward Bill Paterson. He ended the season as top scorer, although it took only eight goals to achieve that, which neatly sums up the plight of Derby's front line.

In March, Derby made another big signing when Harry Storer came from Grimsby Town for £4,500. Storer, a wing-half or inside-forward also played cricket for Derbyshire (as had his father and uncle; his uncle had also played for the Rams). He was joined at the Baseball Ground by Spurs centre-half, Charlie Rance, but both arrived too late to help stave off another relegation. Only five matches were won as Derby went down with Bradford Park Avenue. Quantrill, capped four times for England while with Derby, was a target for several clubs and after the Rams lost their First Division place he moved to Preston. The 1921-22 season was almost as gloomy.

The Rams began with a 4-2 defeat at Blackpool and ended with a 2-0 loss at Rotherham County to finish 12th the Second Division, their lowest-ever final placing in the Football League. The fans voiced their opinions so loudly that the players, tired of the abuse, made a public protest through the *Derby Daily Express*. It made no difference: the fans kept on booing.

Before another season dawned, Derby County had a new manager. In the summer, Jimmy Methven, suffering from glaucoma, entered hospital for what turned out to be an unsuccessful eye operation. It was a sad end to a career that had begun as a player for the Rams back in 1891. Derby

Farcical, foggy trip to Coventry

IN November 1921, Derby County travelled to Highfield Road to meet Coventry City for what already had the look of a relegation battle. But the fans that risked their admission money saw nothing of the game, which lasted barely half an hour – and 30 minutes of farce it was too.

As "County Onlooker" reported in the *Derbyshire Football Express*: "It was a fruitless journey … The fog was so thick that it was almost impossible to discern the band which was discoursing music on the field. In fact, it was impossible from the stand to see more than a yard or two beyond the touchline."

The *Football Express* man was at a loss for anything meaningful to write: "Cheers were heard from different positions on the ground, and all that could be gathered from the first ten minutes' play was that play was being concentrated in the vicinity of the Derby goal."

It was a strange debut for the Rams' George Birdsall, an outside-left from Harpenden Town, who was making his first Football League appearance at the ripe old age of 30. Birdsall, who had just recovered from food poisoning, took the place of the injured John Pattison. Alas, his first league game would not count.

Gradually the fog began to lift and the Rams' goalposts appeared just in time for the crowd to see goalkeeper George Lawrence fist away a corner. A few minutes later, the stand on the opposite side of the ground to the press box loomed into view, and after 20 minutes it was possible to gain a general impression of the game's pattern.

For the Rams, Harry Storer and Jimmy Moore both went close as the sun tried bravely to burn its way through. It was in vain, as the reporter told his readers back in Derby: "… the fog began to creep over the field again and, once more, I had to be content with watching a couple of players – one from each side – running up and down the touchline.

"… Once I just discerned Wightman dribbling away from the centre of the field before punching the ball out to the right … but what the Derby right wing were doing cannot be stated for, although the game had been in progress for half an hour, they did not come into my view, nor that of several hundred other people on the stand where the best seats are situated.

"At the half-hour the players left the field and on enquiry I ascertained that the game had been abandoned, and that there was no score."

Five days later, the Rams returned to Highfield Road and this time the game was played to a conclusion. Scotsman Bill Paterson – who later signed for Coventry – and Frank Keetley, one of nine Derby brothers who all played professional football, scored in their 2-1 win.

advertised the post and on 4 July 1922, just like they would do 45 years later, they appointed a young manager from Hartlepools United. Cecil Potter, a former Norwich City and Hull City forward, was only 33. He brought with him two Hartlepools players, full-back Tom Crilly and centre-half Harry Thoms. In October he also signed a centre-forward, Randolph Galloway from Sunderland Tramways. All three were to give the Rams valuable service and Galloway's goals in particular – 30 in 76 appearances – were most welcome.

But it was Jimmy Moore who achieved the scoring feat of the Rams' season. Against Crystal Palace at the Baseball Ground on Boxing Day, Moore scored five times in a 6-0 win. The same player chipped in with valuable FA Cup goals as Derby knocked out Blackpool, Bristol City, Sheffield Wednesday and Tottenham to reach the semi-finals, where they met fellow Second Division club, West Ham United, at Stamford Bridge. The prize was an appearance in the first FA Cup Final to be staged at Wembley.

At this late stage of the season the Stamford Bridge pitch boasted little grass, but an overnight shower had speeded it up. The weather cleared and, as the teams took the pitch, a watery sun was making a brave attempt to shift the haze which hung over Chelsea's home. The Rams had taken plenty of support but the Hammers silenced the Derby fans with two goals in the first 10 minutes, through Billy Brown and their Jimmy Moore. The opening 10 minutes of the second half were almost a repeat of the first. Moore made it 3-0, and then Brown was presented with the easiest of chances to score number four. Eleven minutes later, the Rams pulled one back when Billy Henderson turned a shot from Derby's Jimmy Moore's into his own net. Three minutes after that, former army footballer Lionel Murphy made the opening and Derby's Moore literally walked the ball into the net past goalkeeper Ted Hufton. But there was to be no sensational fightback. Ten minutes from the end, Ruffell netted West Ham's fifth of the afternoon. The Hammers went on to lose 2-0 to Bolton Wanderers in what became known as the "White Horse" Cup Final. On the same day, the Rams lost 1-0 at home to Leeds United. It would be another 23 years before they trod Wembley's famous turf for the first time.

Derby finished 1922-23 in 14th place in the Second Division – another all-time low – but their reward from the cup run was a share of £6,040 from the semi-final receipts. It went a long way to clearing the club's £10,000 debts, and prompted the Derby board to think about moving to the newly built Municipal Sports Ground on Osmaston Park Road. Plans were drawn up for a 4,000-seater stadium with modern dressing-rooms, gymnasium and offices, but at the club's annual meeting, at the Royal Hotel in July 1924, it was announced that Derby had instead purchased the Baseball Ground from the Ley estate for around £10,000. At that point, Rams fans were still looking back on an exciting season. In late September 1923, Derby lost 3-2 at home to Bristol City. So nobody expected what happened at Ashton Gate seven days later. The Rams won 8-0 to record what is still their biggest away win. Harry Storer scored four and Derby looked a good bet for promotion. Storer had a great season. Moving into the forward line he finished with 24 goals and was capped by England in Paris. When the final day arrived, the Rams needed to beat Leicester by at least 5-0 in order to regain their First Division place on goal-average. Twenty thousand spectators packed into the Baseball Ground and they were rewarded with a match that almost took the Rams home. Moore, Galloway and Storer made it 3-0 at half-time. In the 65th minute, Moore added a fourth. But a fifth goal proved elusive. The Rams missed promotion by 0.015 of a goal.

Supporters were still talking about the near miss when the 1924-25 season opened, and they were in for more thrills. The Rams were never out of the top two. Until, that is, they lost at Stoke with two games to play, and slipped to third. And there they remained. At the end of the season, Cecil Potter announced his retirement from football. He planned to take on a dairy business in his native Sussex but within a week of leaving the Baseball Ground he was manager of Huddersfield Town who he would help complete a hat-trick of Football League championships. The Rams, meanwhile, began to look around for a replacement.

Enter Mr Jobey

ON MAY DAY 1926, Derby County travelled to Edgeley Park for their final match of the season. On the same day, down at St Werburgh's Church, on the corner of Cheapside and Friar Gate, Canon Alfred Blunt was raising eyebrows by preaching what many saw as a pro-socialist sermon. As the nation's trades unions were on the brink of calling a General Strike, the middle-class began to twitch at the thought of the workers revolting. What had happened in Russia was never far from the national psyche in Britain. Of course, there was a General Strike. And although it didn't last long – only a few days in fact – there was violence and the sight of British policemen driving around in armoured cars. In Derby, an emergency centre was set up at the Guildhall, from where volunteers were organised to run the town's essential services. By then, Derby County were back in the First Division. Quite what would have happened if the strike had taken place during the season is anyone's guess. In the 1920s, football matches didn't require the huge police presence of more recent times. But they still needed to be policed and one could hardly imagine they would be a priority if the resources of the civil power had been required elsewhere in such politically volatile times. It is an interesting notion but, while passions ran high back home, the Rams faced a Stockport County team that was about to end an inglorious season bottom of the Second Division. Only 4,000 turned up to watch. Derby had just lost a midweek match at Stamford Bridge – at the hands of promotion rivals, too – so it was a good job that they were already assured of going up. Runners-up to Sheffield Wednesday, they lost 3-0 at Stockport. The Rams new manager had a few words to say afterwards. He was famous for his colourful vocabulary, a man who could spend 10 minutes blistering the ears of an errant player and never repeat himself.

Derby had appointed George Jobey in the summer of 1925. A member of Newcastle United's 1909 League championship and 1911 FA Cup Final teams – and the Arsenal player who scored the Gunners' first-ever goal at Highbury – Jobey managed Wolves to the Third Division North title in 1923-24 before deciding to enter the hotel industry. But the Rams persuaded him back into football.

One of Jobey's first signings was to become a Derby County legend. In September 1925, the Rams paid £3,500 for Blackpool's England international, Harry Bedford, the Football League's leading scorer in 1922-23 and 1923-24. On 3 October, Bedford scored a hat-trick in the Rams' 5-0 win over Swansea Town at the Baseball Ground. It was the first of 27 goals in 31 league games for Bedford that season, and the first of 10 hat-tricks and 152 goals in all senior games in his Rams career. In February, Jobey returned to Bloomfield Road for two more players, inside-forward Jimmy Gill and tiny winger George Mee. The combined fee was £3,500 and, again, it was money well spent. Gill and Mee added impetus to Derby's promotion challenge. There was also a debut for snowy-haired full-back Tommy Cooper, who joined the Rams from Port Vale in March 1926. Cooper cost £2,500, a snip for a player who would become one of the finest defenders of his generation and win 15 caps for England, all of them while with Derby County.

One of the early highlights was a 7-3 win over Stoke City in late October – another Bedford hat-trick – and when Blackpool arrived at the Baseball Ground in January, they were hammered 5-2, even though Bedford missed the game through injury. So, despite that late-season hiccup at Stockport, Derby County returned to the First Division, three points behind champions Sheffield Wednesday and five points ahead of third-placed Chelsea. Like all strikers of the day Bedford enjoyed the first season when only two, not three, defenders were required to play a forward onside. For a few months it liberated the game's goalscorers, at least until Arsenal manager Herbert Chapman reinvented the centre-half as a "stopper" defender.

When supporters arrived at the Baseball Ground on 4 September 1926 for the Rams' first home game in the First Division for five years, they found improvements to the Popular Side terrace had increased the ground's capacity to 30,000. Not that it was needed that day as only 21,461 saw Liverpool beaten 2-1. When the mood took them, Derby scored freely – that season's FA Cup winners, Cardiff City, were beaten 6-3 – but the first success on their travels didn't come until New Year's Day at Upton Park. The win still left Derby in the bottom four and when Sheffield Wednesday arrived at the Baseball Ground on 19 March, relegation was a still a real possibility. But that day proved an amazing one for the Rams. They won 8-0 to embark upon a run-in of 10 games without defeat and a club record haul for a season of 86 league goals. Bedford and Gill ended joint top scorers with 22 each. Jackie Whitehouse, signed from Birmingham in 1923, finished with 13 goals – in that thrashing of Wednesday he scored four – and the ever-reliable Murphy again weighed in with 10. The Rams finished 12th, and that new Baseball Ground capacity had been more than tested for the Boxing Day visit of Bolton Wanderers, when 30,557 fans set a new attendance record.

A poor start to 1927-28 – only one win in the first six matches – was overcome by two splendid unbeaten runs that saw the Rams finish fourth, their best final position since 1897. Again there were some big wins – Blackburn were beaten 6-0, Manchester United 5-0, then poor old Cardiff were again hammered by the Rams – this time 7-1 (Bedford scored four) – who came within four goals of topping a century for the first time. The signing of Aston Villa inside-forward George Stephenson in November proved key. In his first 11 league appearances in a Derby shirt Stephenson scored 12 goals. Going in the opposite direction was goalkeeper Ben Olney. When the Rams beat Villa 5-0 on Boxing Day and 1-0 at Villa Park the following day, they completed their first-ever league double over the Birmingham club. Two days later, Villa signed the out-of-favour Olney – he had lost his place to Harry Wilkes – and within five months the former Rams goalkeeper had been capped twice by England, against France and Belgium.

George Thornewell, the little outside-right who had joined the Rams at the end of the First World War, was also on his way. Unable to regain the place he had lost to Sammy Crooks, signed from Third Division North Durham City in April 1927, Thornewell moved to Blackburn Rovers. Again it was a case of an ex-Ram who prospered. At the end of the season Thornewell was laying on the fastest goal ever scored in an FA Cup Final. Left-back George Collin, who arrived in November 1927 after falling out with Arsenal, was now a regular.

In May 1928, his eyes already on the following season, Jobey signed two more players. The *Derbyshire Football Express* described them as "promising young players … both from Midland League clubs, and both, by coincidence, possessed of the Christian names of John William". Rams supporters would get to know them as Jack Barker and Jack Bowers, legends in the Derby County story.

Centre-half Barker made his debut on 22 December 1928, in a 3-1 home win over Bury. On 2 February 1929, a few days short of his 21st birthday, centre-forward Bowers scored on his first appearance, a 2-1 victory over Bolton Wanderers at the Baseball Ground. One week later he completed a hat-trick at Fratton Park, the second "a goal worthy of Steve Bloomer at his best". That both Bowers and Barker had forced their way into the team so soon after leaving non-League football was a measure of each player's class because this was a great season for Derby County, who in November led the table. Eventually, they fell away to finish sixth but 46 points was the best total they had ever achieved in the First Division. The Rams began 1929-30 with three wins and 10 goals in their first three matches. They ended it as runners-up to Sheffield Wednesday and even though they were 10 points adrift of the champions, as the 1930s dawned, Derby County were becoming a real force.

The Roaring Thirties

On 1 October 1930, Arsenal arrived at the Baseball Ground for a First Division match. Herbert Chapman's Gunners were on their way to the first of four Football League championships in five years. But on that mellow autumn day they took away from Derby nothing more than the taste and smell of Ley's foundry. The FA Cup holders were hit three times in the first 22 minutes as Stephenson, Bedford and Bowers put Derby County into an unassailable lead. Stephenson added a fourth and although Cliff Bastin and Herbert Roberts replied for Arsenal, it was too little too late.

It was the first appearance of the season for Jack Bowers, and how he made up for lost time. By the end of it, the centre-forward had smashed the Rams' individual club scoring record for a season with 37 goals in only 33 matches. He scored four goals each against Chelsea, Portsmouth and Manchester United, and hat-tricks against Sheffield United and Grimsby Town, although the Mariners scored five to win that game at Blundell Park. Crooks scored 15 times – not bad for a winger – and Stephenson 11. If the Rams' defence had been steadier, then Derby would have finished much higher than sixth. In one spell of six matches, Bowers scored 15 goals but the Rams still managed to lose three of them. In December 1930 the prolific Harry Bedford, now 31, was allowed to leave. He signed for Newcastle United. After playing in the five games of the 1931-32 season, 33-year-old Johnny McIntyre, the last link with the Rams' 1923 FA Cup semi-final team, also left the Baseball Ground, for Chesterfield. McIntyre, who captained the 1925-26 promotion team, had given yeoman service to the Rams over 10 years and 369 appearances, a total that would have been even greater but for niggling injuries.

Towards the end of the previous season Stephenson had been sold to Sheffield Wednesday, allowing Peter Ramage, a signing from Coventry City back in 1928, to finally stake a regular place. Mee missed half this season through injury, causing problems for Jobey who now had no consistent performer on the left wing until Aberdeen's Dally Duncan signed in March 1932. Jack Nicholas, son of a pre-war Derby player, was the regular right-half, while Errington Keen was at left-half. Keen, who joined the Rams from Newcastle United in December 1930, took over from Freddie Jessop who broke a leg in the fifth-round FA Cup tie at Maine Road in February 1932, where 10-man Derby lost 3-0. The short cup run was a welcome distraction in a season when the Rams finished a disappointing 15th.

The 1932-33 First Division campaign was brighter – up to seventh place with Bowers top scorer for the third season in a row – but it was the FA Cup that lit up Derby County's season when the quarter-final draw set up two matches of searing quality, the second made possible only by a fluke goal in the dying embers of the first. The Sunderland tie was a major attraction. At the Baseball Ground on 4 March 1933, the teams fought out a spectacular 4-4 draw before a Rams' record crowd of 34,218. Those who had managed to cram themselves in were treated to a breathtaking match, with six goals coming inside the first 36 minutes. Derby went 2-0 in front, through Duncan and Ramage. Sunderland fought back to take a 3-2 lead with goals from Connor, Davies and Gurney. Then it was 3-3, thanks to a fine goal from Bowers. The second half was only four minutes old when Gurney restored Sunderland's lead, but 60 seconds from the final whistle, Duncan hit a sensational equaliser from far out on the left wing.

Years later, at his home in Brighton, Duncan told me: "I meant it as a cross, of course. I was aiming for the far post, meaning it for Sammy Crooks or Jack Bowers. When you saw a left-winger crossing the ball for Derby, it was always to the far post because Bowers got a lot of his goals that way. But this one just happened to float in under the crossbar. Maybe I hit it with the outside of my left foot and it swerved a bit. But as soon as it left my foot, I could see it going in all the way."

Shot or cross, the ball was in the Sunderland net to set up a Wednesday afternoon replay at Roker Park, where the scenes were even more remarkable than the full house at the Baseball Ground. The crowd was over 75,000 – still a record for the ground when Roker was demolished over 60 years later – and there were casualties. Two men died, one in the Shilling Stand after Sunderland had scored an offside goal, one in the crush outside the ground. Several more were injured and thousands locked out, following the progress of the game only through the roars and groans of those wedged inside. Four excursion trains from Derby were turned back when it was realised that the passengers would never gain entry.

The Rams took a more cautious approach to the replay with Jack Bowers playing much deeper than usual as Sunderland, inspired by 19-year-old Raich Carter, poured forward. After 90 minutes there was still no score, but in the 11th minute of extra time, the Rams broke the deadlock with a goal of stunning simplicity. Nicholas swept out a pass to Crooks. The little winger swerved past Shaw and sent over a magnificent centre. Up went Bowers, taking a posse of Sunderland defenders with him, leaving the unmarked Ramage to power a header just inside the far post. There were only two minutes remaining when Jack Kirby – signed from Newhall United in 1929 but until now having found his way barred by the ever-reliable Harry Wilkes – brought off an astonishing save from Davis. With Sunderland fans already shouting "Goal!", Kirby did not just stop the shot, which was going into the top corner – he caught it. Said the *Derby Evening Telegraph*: "Davis got the shock of his life when he saw Kirby make that brilliant save." And that was a far as Derby County went that year. They lost the semi-final against Manchester City, 3-2 at Huddersfield.

As the 1930s progressed, so Derby County maintained their place as one of the best football teams in England. In 1933-34 they finished fourth in the First Division. Bowers was again in superb form – 34 goals from 37 appearances, some coming from his trademark fearless diving headers that took him into areas where other players might have been nervous of sticking their feet. Then disaster struck. The 1934-35 season was barely a month old when Bowers suffered a knee injury that would sideline him for all but two more matches that season. So George Jobey took a risk – he signed Scotland international Hughie Gallacher from Chelsea. There was no doubting Gallacher's genius at both club and international level, but he was a wayward talent. Even a disciplinarian like Jobey might have had his work cut out to control the controversial Scotsman. Supporters need not have worried. Gallacher scored after only six minutes of his debut, behaved himself impeccably at Derby, and by the time he moved on, two years later, had scored 40 goals in only 55 appearances for the Rams. It seemed that Derby County offered a rare period of happiness in a life full of sadness.

Despite his age – he was 31 – the £2,750 fee looked money well spent, for Gallacher had a scoring record every bit as remarkable as that of Bowers. He stood only 5ft 6in – tiny for a leader of the attack – but by the time he arrived at Derby he'd scored 359 goals in 469 matches. He led Newcastle to the First Division title in 1926-27, played in Scotland's Wembley Wizards team that hammered England in 1928, and scored five goals in a match on four occasions, one of them for Scotland in Belfast.

But Gallacher also had a darker side. Married at 17 and divorced at 23, known to like more than a few drinks, and with a string of suspensions behind him, far from solving their scoring problem Gallacher could have spelled trouble for the Rams. Indeed, they had already paid off his debts as part of the transfer deal. Jobey, though, felt that he could handle the player, who moved into a house in Littleover and became friendly with his Scotland teammate, Dally Duncan, who recalled: "Wee Hughie was a charming fellow when he was sober. Jobey just had to keep him off the bottle." It appears that the manager did just that.

By the time the Rams arrived at Blackburn in mid-December 1934, Gallacher had scored four goals in five games for his new club. At Ewood Park it took him 22 minutes to get off the mark, touching home Reg Stockill's downward header after a Crooks corner. Jack Bruton equalised from the penalty spot, but before half-time Gallacher had restored Derby's lead, taking a pass from Crooks before dancing around the goalkeeper. Ernie Thompson levelled the scores again just after the restart, but in the 57th minute, Gallacher screwed the ball home from a tight angle, despite the close attentions of two defenders. Three minutes later, Hughie got his fourth, sidefooting home another Crooks pass, and after Crooks had hit Cliff Binns full in the face with a shot which laid the goalkeeper out, Gallacher whipped the rebound into the net to make it 5-2 after 73 minutes. The *Derby Evening Telegraph* reporter was in raptures: "Hughie Gallacher, the supreme artist in ball control, made goalscoring look the simplest thing in the world … the Scottish international moved along with the ball at his toe as if he had some magical influence over it."

Not surprisingly, Gallacher finished the season as Derby's leading scorer – 24 in 30 games – and topped the list again the following season

Bowers blasts buried United

WHEN newly promoted Manchester United visited the Baseball Ground for the first home match of 1936-37, it was a tale of two high-scoring centre-forwards. Both kept up their remarkable records that day, but only one emerged victorious.

Leading the visitor's attack was Welsh international Tom Bamford, scorer of 175 goals for Wrexham before joining United for whom he was to net another 57.

By the final whistle that September afternoon, Bamford could look back on what would normally have been a successful performance – a hat-trick that had given his side a 3-1 lead.

Jack Bowers, however, went one better. With four goals in 15 minutes he helped the Rams to an astonishing victory. In the first few minutes Derby went ahead with a gift goal. Dally Duncan swung over a corner, Crooks connected with his head and goalkeeper Roy John let the ball slip through his legs; even then it only just rolled over the line before running out of pace.

In the 17th minute, United were level through John Wassell. Then Bamford put the visitors into what should have been an unassailable lead. He scored in the 24th and 28th minutes, and completed his hat-trick six minutes into the second half.

The Rams, who were without England centre-half Jack Barker, missing with a poisoned foot, had Ralph Hann, normally a wing-half, drafted into the middle of the defence. Hann – who became the Rams' trainer in the 1950s, with Jack Bowers as his assistant – struggled out of position as Bamford ran riot.

After 64 minutes Bowers gave the Rams a flicker of hope when he made it 4-2 with a trademark diving header, but it was an injury to United left-back Hugh McLenahan that probably cost Manchester the match.

United had to rejig their line-up, switching right-half Jimmy Brown to look after Derby's flying outside-right, Sammy Crooks. It was a cross from the Rams winger that led to Derby's third goal. John punched the ball out, but only as far as Bowers who hammered it into the net left-footed after 72 minutes.

One minute later Bowers was on target again with another header from a Duncan centre, and the Rams were right back in the game at 4-4.

Eleven minutes from time, it was Bowers again, this time working his way into the penalty area before crashing the ball past John. United were now being run ragged but the scoring had ended and a 21,194 crowd had seen a stunning 5-4 Rams win.

The *Derby Evening Telegraph's* Mark Eaton (the nom-de-plume of reporter Cecil Grounsell) summed up: "Astonishing lapses by the Rams' normally sound defence were the cause of the astonishing score at half-time… Then came one of the most remarkable rallies ever staged by the Rams. A headlong dive, a left-foot shot, another header, then a sprint and a grand drive, all brought goals for Bowers …"

with 16 in 25. He moved to Notts County in September 1936, and ended his career with Grimsby and Gateshead. Alas, Hughie Gallacher, the flawed football genius, met a sad end. On 11 June 1957, on the eve of a court appearance to face a charge of cruelty to his 14-year-old son, he jumped in front of the Edinburgh to York express train near Gateshead. A few days earlier, he had told a journalist: "It's no good fighting when you know you can't win."

With Gallacher in the side, the Rams now had eight internationals – Cooper, Barker, Bowers, Keen and Crooks (England), Duncan and Gallacher (Scotland) and Sid Reid, a reserve-ream full-back who had been capped by Ireland. But then Cooper was sold to Liverpool and that seemed to unsettle the team. At the same time, inside-forward Reg Stockill, who had cost the Rams £2,000 from Arsenal in September 1934, was injured. Stockill had made a storming start with Derby – eight goals in 17 games including a hat-trick in a 9-3 win over West Brom at the Baseball Ground in December – but now he was out until March 1936 and was never again the same player.

In the 1935 close season, the Rams topped-up their quota of internationals by signing Scotland inside-forward Charlie Napier from Celtic. Napier thus resumed his international left-wing partnership with Dally Duncan and the pair helped Derby to another runners-up place in the First Division. The Rams started badly, losing 4-0 at Goodison Park. They ended badly as well, going down 6-0 to Brentford on their first-ever visit to Griffin Park. Yet in between Derby strung together some impressive league victories that were enough to push them into second place, eight points adrift of Raich Carter's Sunderland, and ahead of Huddersfield Town on goal-average. They were still without Jack Bowers, though. He was getting back to full fitness by helping the Rams Reserves win the Central League championship for the first time in their history.

Still the Rams could not scale the very pinnacle. In 1936-37 they slipped back to fourth. Their away form was excellent – only one point short of their record of 21 set in 1934-35 – but they dropped 13 at home, too many for a team with title-winning aspirations. In December 1936, against Charlton Athletic at The Valley, the Rams fielded an all-international forward line: Crooks (England), Dai Astley (Wales), Jack Bowers (England) and Charlie Napier and Dally Duncan (both Scotland). Two years later, almost to the day and on the same ground, they would do so again, with Dave McCulloch (Scotland) and Ronnie Dix (England) replacing Bowers and Napier. Astley had signed from Aston Villa in December 1936; Dix, also from Villa, in February 1937; McCulloch, who had scored four against the Rams in that 6-0 drubbing at Griffin Park in May 1936, came from Brentford in October 1938 for a Rams record fee of £9,500.

In the meantime, the Rams had a wobble, their inconsistencies in 1937-38 – when could finish no higher than 13th – perhaps best summed up by the fact that they managed to lose 7-1 at home to relegated Manchester City who scored 13 goals against Derby that season. Then again, the Manchester side also managed some spectacular inconsistencies of their own. The previous season's Football League champions went down despite scoring more goals than any other team in the division.

It was back up to sixth place for Derby County in 1938-39. By New Year's Eve, the Rams led the table by five points. But supporters knew that it couldn't last. And it didn't. In January, the club perversely sold Dai Astley to Blackpool. Astley told George Jobey that he didn't want to leave. And considering his goals record for the Rams – 49 in 98 appearances – it would have been better to keep him, especially since a fit-again Bowers had been sold to Second Division Leicester. But some talented youngsters were now making their mark at Derby, including wing-half Tim Ward from Cheltenham, and full-back Jack Howe from Hartlepools United. And on 18 March 1939, a young centre-forward called Jack Stamps made his debut, against Charlton Athletic at the Baseball Ground. Stamps, a South Yorkshireman, had caught the eye scoring goals in the Third Division North. He'd begun his Football League career with Mansfield Town who, to their eternal loss, gave him away on a free transfer less than a year later after he had made only one senior appearance for them. Five goals in only 12 matches for New Brighton soon had scouts from bigger clubs taking notice. It was Jobey who moved fastest, paying £1,500 to bring Stamps to the Baseball Ground in January 1939.

The *Derby Evening Telegraph* reporter covering his debut wondered why Jobey had waited so long to use him: "When Derby County signed on John Stamps in January, I was told by an official of the club that this 19-year-old inside-left from New Brighton was good enough to be put in the first team straight away. After his display against Charlton Athletic, whom the Rams defeated by 3-1 on Saturday … I am left wondering why he was not given a chance earlier." The youngster scored twice that day. The next time Charlton's goalkeeper, Sam Bartram, would see Jack Stamps in earnest would be at Wembley in 1946.

The Penalty of War

I T WAS a strange time, that August of 1939 – confusion, contradiction, chaos even. In some ways everything appeared normal. At Nottingham Road, thousands of locals converged on Derby Racecourse for the Bank Holiday meeting where Gordon Richards would ride his usual procession of winners. At the Rutland Ground in Ilkeston, George Pope, a lanky, balding all-rounder from Tibshelf, scored a century to help Derbyshire beat Nottinghamshire. And at the Baseball Ground, Derby County's players tried to ignore the lung-searching smoke that belched from Ley's foundry as they jogged around the narrow cinder track in readiness for another season in the top division of English football.

Elsewhere, things were very different. At the Guildhall in Derby Market Place, council workers were busy moving the town's municipal archives deep underground, along with its art treasures and rare museum exhibits. The celebrated Derby artist, Ernest Townsend, was turning his skills to camouflaging factory roofs and power station cooling towers. And at Friargate railway station, when hundreds of Derbeians left for Skegness (5s 9d return), their children carried not only the usual buckets and spades, but also cardboard boxes. The boxes contained gas masks. Like the rest of Britain, Derby was preparing for war.

Sport, though, was trying to carry on as usual. Back at the Baseball Ground, Derby County's three summer signings were each looking forward to the new season. George Jobey had paid Arsenal £2,000 for Wilf Walsh's signature in the belief that the little outside-right (he stood barely 5ft 5ins tall) might one day take over from Sammy Crooks. Walsh was equally pleased to be at Derby. Although Arsenal had taken him on their tour to Denmark that May, the 22-year-old's first-team chances at Highbury had been severely limited. At 29, Billy Redfern was also happy to have moved to Derby. His 19 goals in 41 appearances for Luton Town had persuaded Jobey that Redfern could be the man to replace Ronnie

Dix, the England international forward who had joined Tottenham. It was quite a step up, from the middle of the Second Division to the top half of the First, but Jobey reckoned that Redfern could do it. Jimmy Wilson's experience had been limited to 36 games for Lincoln City, a club at the wrong end of the Third Division North. But even though he was a year older than Walsh, Wilson was still thought to have potential. And so Wilson, Walsh, Redfern, and all the other Rams players continued to lap around the Baseball Ground. And just to remind them that these times were far from normal, the rest of the town continued to prepare for war. German remilitarisation of the Rhineland in 1936, and Hitler's annexation of Austria in 1938, had been ignored, but when Germany invaded Czechoslovakia in March 1939, another war seemed inevitable.

It had been the same for years: one international crisis after another. As far back as 1934, footballers had been one of the first sections of British society to see for themselves what was happening in Germany. In May that year, when Derby County made a four-match visit, they found a country swathed in swastika emblems. After Hitler's election success the previous year, the Nazi state was firmly established. Dave Holford was a 19-year-old outside-left from Scarborough, excited to be included in the Rams squad despite his lack of experience: "Everywhere we went, the swastika was flying. If you said: 'Good morning,' they'd reply with 'Heil Hitler'. If you went into a cafe and said: 'Good evening,' they would respond with 'Heil Hitler'. Even then, you could see this was a country preparing for war."

Just as the England team would be obliged to do in Berlin four years later, the Derby players of 1934 were ordered to give the Nazi salute before each game. Full-back George Collin, who captained the side when Tommy Cooper left for England duty, recalled their dilemma: "We told George Jobey that we didn't want to do it. He spoke with the directors, but they said that the British ambassador insisted. The Foreign Office were afraid of causing an international incident if we refused. So we did as we were told. All except our goalkeeper, Jack Kirby, that is. Jack was adamant that he wouldn't give the salute. When the time came, he just kept his arm down and turned his back on the dignitaries. If anyone noticed, they didn't say anything."

Unlike the world situation five years earlier when Derby County's players had been in a privileged position to see what was happening in Germany, by August 1939 nobody needed a holiday on the Rhine before they realised the dangers. Throughout the close season, thoughts of war were never far away. Public and domestic air-raid shelters were erected, air-raid precautions exercises held, and the *Derby Evening Telegraph* carried almost daily pleas for more ARP volunteers. The town was 1,000 short of its complement, a fact underlined at Derby police sports day when a race for ARP messengers had to be cancelled when only one entry had been received. Towards the end of August, Derby County started a season they would never finish with a 3-0 defeat at Sunderland. Raich Carter scored twice. On the following Wednesday evening, Portsmouth, the FA Cup holders, were beaten 2-0 at the Baseball Ground, where just over 10,000 spectators saw Redfern and Duncan score the Rams' goals.

On the cricket field, Derbyshire's George Pope was selected for an MCC tour to India. Unfortunately for Pope, the tour would never take place. Other sportsmen would never fulfill their schedule. Two German cars were entered for the late September meeting at Castle Donington. One of the drivers was Manfred von Brauchitsch, a relative of a German general. And although they didn't know it, Derby's horseracing fans had seen their last-ever meeting at the Nottingham Road course.

Through all this, Derby's players trained as usual. They had a match against Aston Villa at the Baseball Ground that Saturday. But it was war that dominated everyone's thoughts. Nine hundred miles away, the 1939 Polish championship had been whittled down to a four-club play-off but the title would never be decided. Warsaw was also preparing itself for war. In Danzig, now the flashpoint of the conflict, bands of Nazis attacked Polish shops, smashing their windows. On Friday, 1 September, the Luftwaffe bombed the Polish capital as German tanks crashed their way over the country's border. In Britain, theatres were closed, cricket matches abandoned, greyhound racing cancelled and the BBC wireless service changed to two wavelengths only. Many amateur football matches were cancelled, but the Football League pressed on for one more Saturday. As the last hours of peace choked painfully away on a sultry afternoon, barely 8,000 supporters bothered to traipse to the Baseball Ground. They saw a match played in a totally unreal atmosphere, for it was now obvious that the result would ultimately count for nothing.

Yet despite that surreal feeling, Derby set off well and McCulloch, Stamps and Duncan all went close in the early stages. As it was, the Rams had to make do with a penalty midway through the second half, when George Cummings bowled over McCulloch. According to the *Derby*

Evening Telegraph, Cummings had "knocked over McCulloch by way of showing his disapproval of the quite legitimate tactics used by the Rams' leader in challenging Rutherford when the goalkeeper was trying to get rid of the ball". In years to come, it would be the forward who would be penalised, but on the first Saturday of September 1939, Jack Nicholas hammered home the penalty kick, low to the goalkeeper's right for the only goal of the game. The sparse crowd trudged out of the Baseball Ground and into the unknown.

Sixty miles away, the mood of the Chesterfield players who had lost to Manchester City was not helped by the sight of barrage balloons on the skyline around Maine Road. That night, the Derby players met at the Anglers' Arms on Nottingham Road in Spondon. The newly built pub had quickly become a favourite post-match venue. As the players sipped their beer, and discussed what the future might hold, a violent thunderstorm raged over Derby and one of the barrage balloons defending the Rolls-Royce aero-engine works near the Baseball Ground was struck by lightning and came crashing down in flames. It seemed an appropriate, almost apocalyptic, backdrop. There was no chance of Germany withdrawing from Poland. "We're out of a bloody job," growled Jack Stamps, wise beyond his 20 years. No one disagreed.

No Cover – No Cup Final

It had been a long war for Derby: 148 air-raid alerts; 45 civilian deaths due to enemy action; 152 high-explosive bombs; 164 incendiary bombs. The heaviest raid came on 15 January 1941, a dreadful night when several people lost their lives. The alert first sounded at 9pm. The all-clear finally rang out at 5.20am. In between, the Luftwaffe dropped 50 high-explosive bombs. The Midland Station and houses at Pear Tree and Normanton were badly damaged. The Baseball Ground did not escape. When the smoke and dust of that long night finally gave way to a bleak dawn, residents in Colombo Street and Shaftsbury Crescent saw that the Osmaston stand had taken a battering. It would be some time before Rams fans would be sitting in there again.

Actually, there was no rush to repair the damage because there was no football to watch. Not in Derby, anyway. After the Football League had been suspended, a few friendly matches were allowed and Derby dipped their toes into the water by arranging a home game against Leeds United. Only 1,805 people turned up. That was enough to convince Derby's directors to shut up shop for the duration. The local Home Guard – Britain's Dads' Army – now did their physical jerks on the grass where Sammy Crooks had once weaved his magic. It was Christmas Day, 1941 before another game was played there: the Rams against the RAF. A few more friendly matches followed, against such diverse opponents at the Belgian Army, and the Pick of the Derby and District Senior League. Attendances improved and when 10,000 sports-starved Derbeians became regulars, Derby County decided that, for the 1942-43 season, they would enter one of the regional competitions that had provided the only real football since 1940.

Even that was hybrid football, with guest players drawn from whoever happened to be stationed in the area. The situation served Derby County well. It brought together two of the greatest players in the club's history. Peter Doherty and Raich Carter, Ireland and England internationals respectively, were both stationed at RAF Loughborough, working with injured airmen. On Saturdays, they starred for the Rams. Carter was the silver-haired playmaker; Doherty the flame-haired trickster. They were considered one of the greatest inside-forward pairings of all time.

When the war ended in August 1945, a transitional season was organised. But the FA Cup was back, albeit with the quirk of every tie up to and including the quarter-finals being played over two legs. As guests, Carter and Doherty were both ineligible for the Cup, so the Rams signed them properly. Derby were fortunate that both men had become disenchanted with their clubs. Doherty had fallen out with Manchester City and had already asked for a transfer; Carter was in a similar position with Sunderland. They were both happy to come to Derby – Carter especially so since his wife was a Chaddesden girl – and in the days of the footballer's maximum wage, they had nothing to lose by switching clubs. They each cost the Rams £6,000 ("Derby were lucky to get me for that," said Carter).

Derby's FA Cup trail began in some style. In the third round the Rams knocked out Luton Town, 9-0 over the two legs. Jack Stamps, the burly forward who on that dark, almost satanic, night of 2 September 1939 had predicted that they were all out of job, scored four times at Kenilworth Road. He'd had an eventful start to his war, had Stamps. Upon the outbreak he'd joined the Royal Artillery and been shipped off to France with the British Expeditionary Force. That had all gone wrong when

Hitler swept through the Low Countries. Stamps found himself waiting on a beach at Dunkirk, looking up at the Luftwaffe and wondering if he would get on one of the small boats that were sailing bravely from England to rescue Britain's beleaguered army. He managed it, just. Although not before one of his own officers had threatened him with a revolver for trying to clamber aboard one of the last little overloaded boats to leave for England.

"If you don't get off, I'll shoot you," said the officer. "Please your bloody self," said Derby County's star-in-waiting. "If you don't the Germans will." And with that, he hauled himself out of the water and fell exhausted on the deck.

When the Rams met West Brom in the fourth round, the crowd was the biggest that the Baseball Ground had seen since 1938. Nearly 32,000 saw a 1-0 win, some of them perched precariously in the bomb-damaged Osmaston stand. It was officially shut but in the chaotic days of post-war Britain, health and safety wasn't even a work in progress. The Rams won the second leg at The Hawthorns, 3-1.

There were also 32,000 at the Baseball Ground for the fifth round when Derby added another six goals without reply to their 4-1 scoreline at Brighton. By the time the Rams reached the semi-final, interest was at fever pitch and the replayed game against Birmingham City at Maine Road attracted over 80,000 fans, still a record figure for a midweek game between English clubs. A young and very nervous Jim Bullions, in at right-half because the elegant Tim Ward was still somewhere in Europe with his field ambulance, recalled having to lift spectators out of the way so that a corner might be taken. This time the Rams made no mistakes, won 4-0, and Wembley beckoned.

Now there were some human stories to tell. Sammy Crooks, the pre-war England winger, would miss the Final. In the sixth-round game at Villa Park, where 76,500 – still the ground record – packed in, Crooks had been the victim of a bone-jarring tackle from Aston Villa's "Mush" Callaghan. He was just about fit again, but the baby-faced Derby-born Reg Harrison kept his place for Wembley. Another local lad would miss out: after playing in almost every game up until then, full-back Jack Parr broke his arm in a Football League South game at Luton. For others there was an unexpected opportunity. Parr's injury opened the Wembley door for Jack Howe, who when the Cup run started had been sailing home from India on a troopship. And when the Rams suffered yet another goalkeeping crisis, Vic Woodley, a former Chelsea and England star, had been brought out of semi-retirement with Bath City.

Derby County now had a different manager from the one with which they had started the Cup campaign. In August 1941 a joint FA-Football League commission had finally got to the bottom of how, throughout George Jobey's time as manager, the Rams could tempt top players to the Baseball Ground. Some inventive accounting had seen the maximum wage structure regularly broken and illegal bonuses paid. Jobey was permanently suspended from football, directors were banned *sine die*, and the club secretary severely censured. The Rams were also fined £500.

All the suspensions were lifted before the end of the war, but when football resumed at Derby in 1941, it was with Jack Nicholas as nominal player-manager although his was never an official position. In March 1944, now settled into wartime regional football, Derby appointed Ted Magner, a former Everton forward and Huddersfield Town assistant manager. Magner was a fine football coach who had worked abroad, and in 1944-45 he guided the Rams to the Football League North title and to the Midland Challenge Cup when Peter Doherty scored five goals against Aston Villa in the Baseball Ground leg of the Final.

In January 1946, after seeing the Rams into the fourth round of the FA Cup, Magner left to coach abroad again, so the directors turned to a former player, Stuart McMillan, who was busy running the Nag's Head pub in Mickleover. McMillan had made one appearance for the Rams before going off to fight with the Derbyshire Yeomanry in the First World War. Now he was in charge of their FA Cup Final team. Older fans can still recite that line-up: Woodley, Nicholas, Howe, Bullions, Leuty, Musson, Harrison, Carter, Stamps, Doherty, Duncan. Leon Leuty and Chick Musson had come up through the ranks, both signing for the Rams as amateurs before the war.

The 1946 FA Cup Final against Charlton Athletic has long entered the annals of Derby County folklore. First there was the threatened players' strike over tickets. Jack Stamps told it best: "The board said that our wives and girlfriends would have to have uncovered seats. Raich and Peter got us together. It was two days before the Final. We were unanimous. We couldn't have our ladies sitting out if it rained when the directors' wives were under cover. So we said: 'No covered seats – no game.' They soon gave in." Then there was the lifting of the "gypsies' curse". In the 1890s, so the story went, a group of gypsies had been turned off the Baseball

Forest felled by five-star Derby

NOTTINGHAM Forest arrived at the Baseball Ground in September 1944, not quite sure what to expect. But then neither did Derby County. Such was the nature of wartime football that the formbook could be thrown out of the dressing room window. The Reds might have held Derby to a goalless draw at the City Ground only seven days earlier, but that counted for nothing.

With team selection a lottery, there had been plenty of bizarre results in wartime. Derby had opened the 1942-43 season with a 6-1 win at Notts County, lost 8-1 at Wolves in November, and two months later beat Mansfield Town 10-0.

A lot depended on who was on leave and who was stationed nearby. Defender Jack Nicholas had to play in goal at Barnsley in September 1944. First-choice Frank Boulton was stranded in Birmingham and his replacement arrived at Derby bus station a few minutes after the Rams' transport had left. That season the Rams used ten goalkeepers.

The League North was a complicated affair. It was split into two periods either side of Christmas, and there was also a War Cup that had both qualifying and knockout stages. Occasionally the same match counted in two different competitions. Mostly, people went along just to enjoy some football.

And there was plenty to enjoy when Forest arrived for the second game of the 1944-45 season. In goal for the Rams was a local player, Ray Bilton. Burnley's John Marshall and Flying Officer Reg Trim, originally on Forest's books, were the full-backs. The future Cup-winning half-back line of Jim Bullions, Leon Leuty and Chick Musson was in place. Former England winger Sammy Crooks was on the right, partnered by Tommy Powell who, three years earlier, had been playing for Bemrose School. The left-wing pairing was another future Cup-winning combination: Peter Doherty and Dally Duncan.

At centre-forward, however, the Rams had a stand-in. Fred Tapping, a local man, had been playing in Blackpool's half-back line, behind Stan Mortensen and Stan Matthews. Tapping had played in the previous match, at the City Ground, as a right-half, but on this day he had been drafted in to lead the attack.

He did it with such effect that Forest were overrun. Five goals went past goalkeeper Lawrie Platts, three of them scored by Tapping, with Powell and an own-goal from a Forest defender completing the rout.

Tapping played for the Rams until November and enjoyed a fine record of ten goals in only nine games. At the end of the war he moved from Blackpool to Chesterfield, for whom he made his only Football League appearance, in 1947-48.

Fred Tapping also made a name for himself as a local cricketer with Rolls-Royce in Derby, no doubt never short of the offer of a drink when anyone discovered that he had once scored a hat-trick against Nottingham Forest.

Ground, so they cursed the club never to win a major honour. In the next half-century the Rams had only three losing FA Cup Finals to show for their efforts. But the club had apparently enjoyed a cordial relationship with the gypsies. One of them, "Old Mallender", was even employed to roll the pitch. Nevertheless, an enterprising journalist took Jack Nicholas to a gypsy camp, silver crossed a Romany palm, and the curse was lifted. That did the trick, but only after more drama.

The 1946 FA Cup Final was still looking for its first goal when Charlton half-back Bert Turner diverted a shot from Peter Doherty into his own net. There were only 10 minutes to go and Derby hearts leapt. But two minutes later, Turner took a free-kick and this time the ball brushed Doherty's shins, giving Woodley no chance. So, had Turner scored for both sides? Or had Doherty scored for both sides? The only indisputable fact was that the score stood at 1-1. Now another piece of FA Cup folklore: the ball burst. With five minutes remaining, Stamps shot and might have scored the winner but, as he succinctly put it: "The bloody thing just went 'phut'." Wartime footballs were always bursting. The Japanese invasion of Malaya in 1942 meant that rubber was a rare commodity and better spent on things like aircraft production than football manufacture. But it was another good story. And so was extra time, at least so far as Derby County were concerned. Stamps had two more shots, the ball didn't burst again and both ended up in the net. So did an effort from Peter Doherty, which meant that the final score was Derby County 4 Charlton Athletic 1. Jack Nicholas received the trophy from George VI, little Reg Harrison couldn't take his eyes off his medal, and a few days later, tens of thousands of happy Derby County supporters packed the streets of the town to see the Cup paraded on an Offiler's beer dray. Eventually, Nicholas held it aloft from the balcony of the police station in Full Street (the Council House, started in 1939, was still only partially built and the Air Ministry had commandeered the usable bit).

At the end of the season, the Rams arranged a tour to Czechoslovakia and Austria. Raich Carter was going to miss the Czech part of the trip. He had been selected to play for England in Paris and would join his Derby teammates in Vienna. But after the international, he received a telegram. He was to fly to Prague instead. The Derby players had been expected to journey to Austria aboard army lorries. The Derby directors refused, the Austria leg was cancelled, and instead, an extra game arranged in

Prague, against a combined Sparta and Slavia team. From the kick-off of the hastily arranged match the hosts tore into the Derby players. They were well supported by some biased refereeing. Foul after foul went unpunished. Eventually, a Czech player held down Vic Woodley while his teammate rolled the ball into the net. The Rams players surrounded the referee, who indicated that he couldn't understand what they were saying, and the goal stood. Then Derby got the ball fairly in the net and, to their intense surprise, the goal was allowed to stand.

Ten minutes into the second half, scores of spectators rushed on to the pitch. They were after Peter Doherty, who had narrowly evaded a crude tackle and then watched as his would-be assailant overbalanced and took a tumble himself. The Czech reserves were first on to the pitch, closely followed by a section of the crowd. Eventually, the local police sauntered on and calmed things down. Raich Carter said afterwards that it was the worst game in which he'd ever played: "It was a good job that it was the last one of the tour because I'd have refused to play in another." Happily, he was to play in plenty more for Derby County.

Grateful To Be Playing Again

FOR OVER a million Britons there was only one place to be on Saturday, 31 August 1946 – at a Football League ground. The days when football matches were interrupted by air-raids, and teams made up their numbers by borrowing from their opponents, or even from the crowd, were over. Now there were no guest players, but there was promotion and relegation. Now there was a return to the old ways of football.

The fixture list was a replica of that for 1939-40. So on the opening day Derby County travelled to Sunderland where a crowd of 48,466 greeted them. In September 1939, Derby had lost 3-0. This time they did slightly better but still came away with nothing. A goal from Stamps and a Doherty penalty weren't enough because Sunderland still scored three. The following Wednesday there were 21,797 at the Baseball Ground when Carter and Stamps earned the Rams a 2-0 win – the same scoreline as seven years earlier – and 28,454 for the following home match, against Aston Villa. On the eve of war in 1939, Jack Nicholas's penalty was the only goal of the game. This time Raich Carter scored the Rams' goal but Villa replied with two.

In September the Rams signed Frank Broome, Villa's versatile goalscorer. Derby paid a transfer fee of £5,000, and they desperately need a player of Broome's calibre. Cup-winner Reg Harrison was injured, forcing the veteran Sammy Crooks, now full-time chief scout but semi-retired player, to turn out again. Crooks played three games before retiring for good.

The most capped England player between the wars, apart from Arsenal's Eddie Hapgood, Crooks had played 445 senior games for

Derby and scored 111 goals. And that despite losing seven seasons to the war, as had so many of his generation.

He was one of several great Rams names now bowing out. In October, Dally Duncan was transferred to Luton Town, and on Boxing Day, Peter Doherty made his last appearance in a Derby shirt. Doherty wanted to take over the licence of the Arboretum Hotel near the Baseball Ground but the Rams directors objected ("They said it would affect my football. That showed that they didn't know me so I had to leave. But I loved Derby.").

In January 1947 the Rams began their defence of the FA Cup, against Bournemouth. On a waterlogged Dean Court pitch, goals from Ward (playing as a makeshift left winger) and Carter sent Derby through to the fourth round and an away tie against Chelsea. When they earned a goalless draw at Stamford Bridge, the Rams must have felt that the hardest part of their task had been accomplished. But when a foolhardy act saw their goalkeeper, Alec Grant, go off injured after only four minutes of the replay, it looked likely that the trophy would slip from Derby's grasp after all. Rams fans need not have worried. Two outstanding performances, one from centre-half Leon Leuty, one from stand-in goalkeeper Frank Broome, paved the way for a nail-biting victory on an ice-bound pitch.

It also left Broome with a tale that he never tired of retelling. Over 40 years later, the former Rams forward was still only too ready to recount the day he denied one of England's most feared goalscorers for almost two hours: "Alec Grant had a habit of doing a little hop, we called it hitch-kicking, when he cleared the ball out of his hands. As we were in the tunnel, the manager, Stuart McMillan, told him to be careful of the bone-hard pitch. I can hear him now: 'Remember Alec, no hitch-kicking today.' Blow me, we'd been going less than five minutes when Alec caught the ball and did his party-piece. Down he went, and dislocated his elbow. There were no subs in those days so, apart from having no goalkeeper, we were also down to 10 men. I volunteered to go in straightaway because I liked keeping goal in training. I really fancied it. A chance to be a hero."

In training, though, Broome did not have to face the likes of England centre-forward Tommy Lawton. But for the next 116 minutes, the stand-in 'keeper kept Lawton and his fellow Chelsea forwards at bay.

After 25 minutes, Grant returned, his elbow heavily strapped, and went on the left wing. The injured goalkeeper was far from a passenger, though, and in the tenth minutes of extra-time, with the game still goalless, he swung over a long crossfield pass to Reg Harrison on the opposite wing. Harrison pushed a pass down the centre for Jack Stamps to take in his stride. Stamps tricked centre-half Harris, brushed off another challenge, and then lobbed the ball over goalkeeper Harry Medhurst. It was a superb goal and it won the game for Derby. In the next round, however, the Rams lost their grip on the Cup. They went down 1-0 before a 44,000 crowd at Anfield, where the prolific Jack Balmer scored Liverpool's goal. The Chelsea replay remained the highspot of Derby's season – they finished 14th in the league – and years later, whenever Frank Broome saw Tommy Lawton, he would extend a hand and say: "Tommy, shake hands with the only goalkeeper you never scored against!"

Thanks to one of the worst winters in living memory, the 1946-47 season dragged on to the very last day of May, by which time the Rams had said farewell to another pre-war stalwart. In April, Cup Final skipper Jack Nicholas played his final game. Bert Mozley, a youngster from Chester Green, would now wear the right-back shirt for Derby County.

The Rams could again boast one of the best teams in the land, and in June 1947 they strengthened it further by paying a British record fee of £15,000 for Morton's Scotland international inside-left, Billy Steel. Steel had burst upon the scene with a scintillating performance for Great Britain against the Rest of Europe at Hampden Park. But his presence would have an unsettling effect on the Derby dressing room. His wages were topped up by an outside "job" with a business belonging to one of the Rams directors, and when other players still travelled to the Baseball Ground by Corporation bus, Steel rolled up in his motor-car. His wispy smile also hid a dark side to his character. Frank Broome recalled answering his own front door in Littleover's Hillsway one day to find Steel's two brothers-in-law looking for the Scot to "sort him out" after a domestic incident involving Steel's wife.

Steel's colleagues felt that he wasn't a team player, reserving his best performances for afternoons when the London press were reporting on the match, or when the Scotland selectors were watching. It led to several players leaving Derby. Angus Morrison, a forward who couldn't abide his fellow Scot, went to Preston North End and played for them in the 1954 FA Cup Final. England full-back Jack Howe was no fan of Steel, either. He moved to Huddersfield Town. Another England player had no problem with Steel, however. As a nursing orderly with the

15th Scottish Division, Tim Ward had seen action in Normandy from D-Day onwards and had been one of the first Allied soldiers to enter Belsen concentration camp "Billy Steel? I was just grateful to be playing football again," Ward said.

In 1947-48, the Rams finished fourth in the First Division. When that season's champions, Arsenal, arrived at the Baseball Ground in November, looking to extend their unbeaten run of 17 matches from the start of the season, Derby played them off the park and were worth more than the Harrison goal that won them the game. There was also a remarkable match at Preston, where the score was 4-4 with only 17 minutes remaining before a Tom Finney-inspired home team won 7-4. Morrison's hat-trick for the Rams that day no doubt oiled his move to Deepdale a year later. Derby County were also one of the favourites to win the FA Cup that season. In the semi-final they faced Manchester United, a club rejuvenated under Matt Busby. The game at Hillsborough was an anticlimax for the Rams. Steel scored for Derby, but Stan Pearson struck a hat-trick for United, and the Rams went out with no complaints. Manchester United went on to beat Blackpool in what became regarded as one of the great FA Cup Finals.

Playing for United that day was inside-forward Johnny Morris. In April 1945, as United's season in the Football League North drifted to a close, Morris had been engaged elsewhere, crossing the Rhine with the Royal Armoured Corps. Tim Ward had been in the neighbourhood with the 51st Highland but the two didn't meet. They were to become friends, though. In March 1949, Derby County broke the British transfer record for the second time in less than two years when they paid Manchester United £24,500 to bring Morris to the Baseball Ground. He came to fill the void left by Raich Carter, who a year earlier had been allowed to take up the post of player-assistant manager with Hull City. The Rams hoped that the Morris-Steel pairing would prove to be another "Carter-Doherty". Morris certainly made a blazing start to his Derby career, scoring 13 goals in his first 13 appearances, including hat-tricks against Charlton Athletic and Stoke City. It was form that won him an England place as Derby won six of their last seven matches, draw the other, and finished third, five points adrift of champions Portsmouth and behind runners-up Manchester United only on goal-average.

The one thing this Derby County team lacked was consistency. In 1949-50 they slipped to 11th. There were still some highlights, like beating relegation-doomed Manchester City 7-0. The German Bert Trautmann, former paratrooper and prisoner-of-war, was making one of his first appearances for City. Five weeks later, the Rams slammed another five past City in the FA Cup at Maine Road. Derby then won a replay against Bury before Northampton Town were the visitors for a fifth-round tie. The attendance that day – 38,063 – broke the Baseball Ground record. Northampton brought an estimated 10,000 supporters in six special trains and 100 motor coaches, all hoping to see the Cobblers improve on what was promising to be their best-ever cup run. At just before 1pm on that second Saturday of February 1950, Derby County's 24-year-old outside-right, Tommy Powell, hurried down Portland Street on his way to the Baseball Ground. Under his flat cap, and with his raincoat collar turned up against the biting wind, Powell did not stand out among the thousands pouring towards the ground. Certainly at least one disconsolate supporter failed to recognise him. As he trudged away from the ground, the fan told Tommy: "I shouldn't bother mate. You'll never get in." "Well, I'll have a go," laughed the Rams winger. It was as well he did. Powell was a major contributor in the Rams winning 4-2. The attendance was the biggest since January 1936 when 37,830 had packed in to see the Rams play Nottingham Forest – yet when Derby met Everton at home in the quarter-finals, there was a crowd of only 32,128 to see the Rams lose 2-1.

In March 1950, another member of the FA Cup-winning team moved on when Bradford Park Avenue paid £20,000 for Leon Leuty. Leuty was another of those unsettled by Billy Steel. If he had waited a few months he would outstayed the little Scot. In September 1950, Dundee paid the Rams a Scottish record fee of £23,000 for Steel. Frank Broome had also left the Baseball Ground. After 45 goals in 112 league appearances, he joined Notts County.

In November 1949, the football authorities again caught up with Derby County's inventive bookkeeping. The offences went back to the post-war transitional season of 1945-46 when PAYE had not been deducted from players' wages, and illegal close-season payments had been made for the end-of-season trip to Czechoslovakia. Chairman Ben Robshaw (the only 1945-46 director still in office) and club secretary Jack Catterall were suspended *sine die* and the club fined £500.

It was 11th place again for the Rams in 1950-51, the most memorable day of that season coming on 16 December when Derby and Sunderland played out an 11-goal thriller on an icy, snow-covered Baseball Ground pitch. Johnny Morris was the star of the show – "He put Rudolph the Red-Nosed Reindeer to shame," declared the *Derby Evening Telegraph* – but when it came to star billing in this football pantomime, another player wasn't far behind. Centre-forward Jack Lee had joined the Rams in June 1950, for £18,500 from Leicester City, with Stuart McMillan predicting that, if he signed for the Rams, then Lee would play for England. Four months later Lee was scoring on his international debut, in Belfast. On this day he scored four times as the Rams won 6-5. At the end of the season Derby and Sunderland both had 40 points, the Rams just shading it on goal-average, thanks in part to that remarkable December day at the Baseball Ground.

By 1951-52, the great Derby County team of the 1940s was breaking up fast. Of those remaining from the 1946 Cup-winning side, only Reg Harrison was still a regular. Wembley goalscorer Jack Stamps played in just over half the games, while Chick Musson managed only 11 appearances. Tim Ward had also left, joining Barnsley, and his right position was shared between Steve McLachlan, an eternal reserve who had been on the Rams' books since 1938, and local youngster Albert Mays. Ken Oliver, from Sunderland, took Leuty's place, and other locally produced players stepping up included full-back Geoff Barrowcliffe from Ilkeston Town, another Ilkeston product in centre-forward Ray Straw, and Derby-born Jack Parry. Chesterfield's long-serving goalkeeper, Ray Middleton, now with the Rams, played in every game. Each would serve Derby well, but the days of a team packed with internationals were over as the Rams flirted with relegation before finishing 17th.

It was a temporary stay of execution. In 1952-53, Derby County finished bottom of the table to face Second Division football for the first time since 1926. The Rams scraped only three points from their first eight games. In October, Morris moved to Leicester City, a club he would eventually help out of the Second Division, and although the Rams paid Wolves £15,000 for inside-forward Jimmy Dunn, and even though Dunn marked his debut with a goal, Derby never recovered from their poor start. It was down, and down again. The Rams made no new signings and the summer of 1953 was marked only by the departure of goalkeeper Bill Townsend and the veteran Steve McLachlan. Like McLachlan, Townsend was a survivor of Derby County's pre-war days but had never been able to establish a regular place, making only 93 appearances in seven peacetime seasons before dropping into the Birmingham League with Burton Albion. In December 1953, after 126 goals in 262 games, Jack Stamps left for Shrewsbury Town.

The return to the Second Division saw some woeful performances as the Rams finished 18th, only five points from relegation. In November 1953, Stuart McMillan stepped down. The board appointed Jack Barker, the Rams great pre-war England centre-half. Alas, fine Rams player that he was, Barker was an unsuccessful manager at Derby. Despite spending £40,000 on players like Bury's Scottish winger Stewart Imlach, former Wolves and England centre-forward Jesse Pye, Celtic goalkeeper George Hunter, and Hull City forwards Alf Ackerman and Ken Harrison, he failed to keep the Rams up. Bert Mozley had seen the way the wind was blowing and had already said farewell, sailing for Canada a few days after his final appearance, against Notts County in December 1954. He was well out of it. A run of seven successive defeats in March and April 1955 – part of a 14-match spell without a win – doomed Derby County to Third Division football for the first time in their history. Inevitably, that meant the end of Jack Barker's brief tenure as manager.

That Man Was Harry Storer

I T IS hard to imagine that Derby County, even in their darkest hours, ever worried about the counter-attraction of Derbyshire cricket. In August 1955, however, as the Rams faced their first-ever season in the Third Division North, kick-off on the opening Saturday was put back until evening because the club feared that many supporters were more likely to choose Derbyshire's match against Gloucestershire over a visit from Mansfield Town. Derby's final home game of the previous season had seen less than 8,000 fans turn up for the visit of Hull City. Now, only nine seasons after winning the FA Cup, the Rams had fallen so far from grace that their fixture list featured the likes of Workington, Barrow and Southport.

From a list of 43 applicants the Rams chose Harry Storer, their former player and England international, to the task of halting the club's alarming slide. Storer had a good managerial pedigree: he had taken Coventry City up to the Second Division in 1936, and Birmingham to the First in 1948. He made two important pre-season signings for the Rams, each reflecting the way he would style his team for the fight back. From West Brom came the skilful Irish international midfield player Reg Ryan, for £3,000; from Coventry, Storer brought Martin McDonnell, a rugged ex-paratrooper centre-half who had twice before been signed by Storer, for Birmingham and for the Highfield Road club. Most of all Harry Storer wanted commitment. When the Rams' team coach left for an away game, he would always punch his chest and ask: "How many hearts have I got with me today?"

On Saturday, 20 August 1955, Derbyshire – third in the County Championship in 1954 and riding high again this season – certainly gave value for money. New skipper Donald Carr scored 139 and eventually declared his side's innings closed at 329 for seven. Then the bowlers struck and Gloucestershire were soon in trouble. How many spectators left early to rush to the Baseball Ground is not known, but when Ryan, an FA Cup winner with West Brom the previous year, led out the Rams at just before 7pm, the players were amazed to find a crowd of over 24,000 waiting to greet them. Derby enjoyed a comfortable win. Ackerman scored twice, Pye and Mays, once each, and the Rams were away to a 4-0 start. On the Monday, Derbyshire completed their rout of Gloucestershire's first innings – all out for 47 with Cliff Gladwin returning figures of 7-13. Following-on, Gloucestershire lost by an innings and 36 runs.

So, Derby's fears that attendances would fall away were unfounded. Several times the 20,000 mark was broken at the Baseball Ground, and when Grimsby Town arrived in March 1956, over 33,000 saw the promotion battle. Grimsby won 3-1 but the key moment in the Rams' season came when Jack Parry had to the leave the field with a serious back injury after clashing with Grimsby full-back, Ray de Gruchy. Parry had scored 24 league goals, but he did not play again that season. Only one club was promoted and, without Parry's goals, Derby finally trailed the Mariners by five points.

On the eve of the following season, Ray Straw's brother offered him half a crown (13p) for every goal and 10 shillings (50p) for every hat-trick. A record-equalling 37 goals and three hat-tricks saw Straw collect over a fiver. It might have been more. When Accrington Stanley visited the Baseball Ground in March 1957, only the woodwork prevented him from scoring the winner with a last-minute header. The loss of a home point to promotion rivals was disappointing but with seven victories in their final 10 matches the Rams lifted the title four points ahead of Hartlepools United, with Accrington a further point behind.

On Easter Monday, Chesterfield were the visitors. Three days earlier the sides had drawn 2-2 at Saltergate but on this day the Rams were in superb form, A near-30,000 crowd saw them win 7-1 with Straw's third hat-trick of the season leaving him three short of overtaking the club record set by Jack Bowers in 1930-31. On the following Saturday, the Rams made sure promotion by beating Southport 2-0 at the Baseball Ground. Straw got both goals, now leaving him just the game at York on the Monday to break the record. In the 1-1 draw at Bootham Crescent

Day to forget against Boston's Derby old boys

WHEN the football results began to splutter from newspaper teleprinters across Britain on a murky Saturday afternoon in December 1955, sub-editors probably decided to ignore the score coming from the Baseball Ground. The glaring error would soon be corrected. Clearly, the operator at the other end had muddled the teams.

But the correction never came. One of the most astonishing scorelines in the history of the FA Cup was indeed correct. Boston United of the Midland League had defeated Derby County, Cup winners only nine years earlier but now Third Division North newcomers, 6-1.

The story did not end there. Boston fielded no less than six former Derby County players. Managed by ex-Rams goalkeeper Ray Middleton, they included 1946 Cup winner Reg Harrison and four more ex-Derby players. Centre-forward Ray Wilkins, a schoolteacher, had scored 11 goals in 30 league games for the Rams. Don Hazledine had managed 28 appearance and six goals; his brother, Geoff, had played once. Centre-half Dave Miller had also appeared just once for Derby, remarkably, though, as a makeshift centre-forward between Raich Carter and Billy Steel.

From the start, Boston – with derisive chants of "Derby old boys" ringing in their ears – tore into the Rams. After 26 minutes they took the lead. Harrison's shot cannoned off Frank Upton, and Wilkins hooked the ball past Terry Webster in the Derby goal. The majority of the 23,767 crowd were surprised but not unduly worried at this stage. Seven minutes later they were beginning to panic.

Wilkins chased a long ball and helped it on to Howlett. Webster got a hand to his shot, but the ball rolled free and Geoff Hazledine made it 2-0. Although former Wolves and England inside-forward, Jesse Pye, scored from the penalty spot, Boston were soon back on the attack and before half-time had restored their two-goal lead.

Webster and Martin McDonnell got into a terrible tangle over Howlett's cross and Johnny Birbeck rose to head Boston's third.

Derby emerged for the second half without the injured McDonnell, and their ten men were no match for rampant Boston. Geoff Hazledine linked up with Wilkins for two carbon-copy goals to complete his hat-trick. And 12 minutes from time, Wilkins took a pass from Harrison and dribbled around Webster to complete an astonishing rout.

Reg Harrison said: I've never known a half-time like it. No one sat down. We just wanted to get at them again. The game can be summed up by one incident: I gave Albert Mays ten years and ten yards, and still got to the ball first. "Afterwards I went into the Derby dressing-room to commiserate and it was deserted except for Harry Storer, the manager, and Ralph Hann, the trainer. Harry just looked at me, blank-faced, and said: 'You can clear off for a start.' Only it was quite a bit stronger than that."

he failed to find the net, although his heart must have been in his mouth when the referee awarded a penalty and then changed his mind.

In all, the Rams scored 111 league goals – one more than the previous season – and many of Straw's 37 were created by wingers Tommy Powell and Dennis Woodhead, both of whose class shone out against Third Division defenders. Woodhead, who had been involved in two Second Division promotions with Sheffield Wednesday, cost Derby £1,500 when he was transferred from Chesterfield in January 1956, and besides laying on goals for Straw, he also scored 14 himself in 1956-57. In January 1957, the supporters' association paid £5,150 to bring Scunthorpe United's Gordon Brown to Derby. He repaid them nine goals in his 17 appearances during the vital run-in.

Harry Storer had worked wonders in his first two seasons back at the Baseball Ground. Reg Ryan, recalled: "Whichever club I signed for, I always chose it for the man who managed it rather than the club itself. At Derby that man was Harry Storer."

It was up to skipper Ryan to steady things on the field after the Rams faced Second Division opposition again in August 1957. The season started badly for Derby – losing 2-0 at Fulham on the opening day, then 5-2 at Bristol Rovers in midweek, followed by a 4-0 hammering at the hands of Barnsley in the first home game. On the following Wednesday, the Rams met Bristol Rovers in the return fixture. Out went Ray Straw, hero of the promotion season, and in came little George Darwin, a mercurial inside-forward signed from Mansfield Town in May. McDonnell returned to the centre of the defence where Storer had given an early opportunity to the stylish but less aggressive Ray Young. The changes did the trick: Darwin and Parry, now happily back to something like full fitness, scored, and the Rams had their first win on the board, 2-1.

In October, Storer decided that Straw wasn't going to score goals at this level. The man who 12 months earlier had been tearing Third Division defences apart was going back there, this time to Coventry City in the Southern Section. At the end of November the Derby career of another promotion regular, goalkeeper Terry Webster, also came to an abrupt end. After conceding seven goals in two games – four of them at home to Huddersfield Town for whom 17-year-old Denis Law scored a penalty – Webster was replaced by Norwich City's Ken Oxford, who the Rams had turned down after a trial back in 1948. The holiday matches produced some strange results. After losing 2-1 to Bristol City on Christmas Day,

Derby beat the same opposition 5-2 on Boxing Day. And when a 1-0 Easter Monday home win over Swansea Town finally banished relegation fears, perhaps the Derby players were too relaxed 24 hours later when they ran out at Vetch Field where Ivor Allchurch's hat-trick helped the Swans sink the Rams 7-1. Still, considering their dreadful start, Derby could be pleased – perhaps relieved is a better word – with their 16th-place finish.

Seventeen games into 1958-59, however, relegation talk was again in the air. The Rams had collected only 13 points, which put them 17th in the table. None of the new faces – centre-forwards Ralph Hunt (from Norwich City) and Peter Thompson (from Hartlepool United), and wingers Dave Cargill (Sheffield Wednesday), Johnny Hannigan (Sunderland) and Ray Swallow (Arsenal) – had changed the Rams' fortunes early on. The turning point of the Rams' season came on 29 November when they beat Charlton 3-2 at the Baseball Ground to embark upon a run that saw them lose only five more games that season. Fifteen wins in the last 23 matches took Derby up to seventh place. With that kind of finish, even an average start would have seen them challenging for promotion.

Powell and Darwin had both enjoyed purple patches, while Parry's 15 goals saw him head the scorers to signal a return to the form that had eluded him since his back injury three seasons earlier. Big Les Moore, signed from Midland League football and continuing to combine part-time football with his job as an insurance agent, was a rock at centre-half. And we mustn't forget Glyn Davies who took over the captaincy when Ryan left for Coventry City just after the season began. Davies wasn't the most skilful player but he was the fiercest – in January 1959 he was sent off for a dreadful tackle on Sheffield Wednesday's Alan Finney at Hillsborough – and his wholehearted commitment spurred on his teammates.

The Rams had also enjoyed some FA Cup spice in 1958-59 when they met Preston North End at the Baseball Ground. Twice they led the First Division high-flyers before Albert Mays tried an ill-advised 30-yard back-pass on a rutted, snowbound pitch. It turned into the perfect through-ball for Dennis Hatsell to equalise. In the *Derby Evening Telegraph*, Wilf Shaw reported: "A stranger to both teams would surely have picked wrongly if asked to identify which was challenging for the First Division title." But the Rams still went out in the Deepdale replay.

There were more new faces at the Baseball Ground in 1959-60. Manchester City's Irish international winger, Fionan "Paddy" Fagan, was the most experienced. Fagan was signed just before the March transfer deadline for £7,500. Huddersfield Town full-back Tony Conwell cost £6,000 in the 1959 close season. And young forwards Ian Buxton and Ian Hall – like Swallow both Derbyshire cricketers – and John Bowers, son of the great goalscorer, Jack, were also introduced. Alas, a season that began with such hope quickly degenerated into despair. In only their second home game Derby lost 7-1 to Middlesbrough for whom, remarkably, the prolific Brian Clough didn't manage to score. Relegation fears were not banished until the penultimate game and the Rams finished 18th. One memory to be taken away from that season was the visit of Manchester United in the FA Cup. Over 33,000 saw United win 4-2 but the Rams played well against star-studded opposition.

Only the signing of Brighton centre-forward Bill Curry, for whom the Rams paid £12,000, the biggest transfer fee they had laid out in years, lit up the 1960-61 season. Curry, a former Newcastle and England under-23 player, gave the crowd someone to cheer and they cheered every one of his 19 goals. Another new signing, Chesterfield's Barry Hutchinson saw £2,250 plus Mays and Martin going in the opposite direction. Hutchinson was never a crowd favourite but 16 goals in his first season were welcome.

On the Wednesday evening of 22 April 1961, supporters flocked to the Baseball Ground to say goodbye to Tommy Powell. After more than 400 appearances and 63 goals for Derby County, the local lad whose first appearance had been as a 16-year-old against the RAF on Christmas Day 1941, had decided to call it a day. Injury ruled out a farewell appearance so Powell was introduced to the crowd and then shook hands with his clubmates, who marked the occasion by losing 3-2. In fact they lost their last four games to finish 12th. Powell was pressed back into action almost as soon as the 1961-62 season started. He made five appearances – and scored another goal – before a crude tackle in a League Cup match against Portsmouth on a damp October evening at the Baseball Ground finally ended a great Derby County career.

The season had started so promisingly for the Rams who by the middle of December were joint second in the table, even without Frank Upton who in August had been sold to Chelsea for £15,000. Notts County outside-right Don Roby, Coventry's former England goalkeeper Reg Matthews, and Chesterfield forward Keith Havenhand all appeared to have joined a promotion-chasing team. But the second half of season was a dreadful affair. After Christmas the Rams managed to win only three games to finish 16th. The main highlight had come in October when high-flying Liverpool lost 2-0 at the Baseball Ground. One Rams goal was a spectacular affair, a long-range shot from local youngster Mick Hopkinson. Bill Curry – he would finish leading scorer again, this time with 25 league and cup goals – was clattered into the Popular Side railings, and there was crowd trouble inside the ground and at Derby Midland station. "Soccer's Day Of Shame," boomed the *Daily Mail*. When the last day of the season arrived, only 6,739 bothered to watch the Rams beat already doomed Brighton 2-0. It was the lowest Baseball Ground attendance since 5,937 saw Luton Town in March 1955. There was one bright spot: in March, Harry Storer had given a debut to an 18-year-old wing-half from Belper. Ron Webster would share in some of the greatest days in Derby County's history.

A Younger Man is Needed

I N MAY 1962, Harry Storer handed in his resignation. Storer was 64. He had been in management for 31 years. "A younger man is needed," he said, "one who is able to deal with the worries, frustrations and hard work that are part and parcel of a football manager's life." Worries, frustrations and hard work or not, there were 52 men who wanted his job. His successor was not among them, however. Tim Ward, a stylish wing-half for the Rams in the post-war years, did not apply. He was still reflecting on the fact that he had just guided Grimsby Town to promotion from the Third Division. But he was the man that Derby County wanted. Chairman Fred Walters approached Ward, who was not bound by a contract with Grimsby, and he accepted. "I always loved Derby," he said. So he took the job for £2,500 a year and Vauxhall Victor car.

After he arrived at the Baseball Ground towards the end of June, Ward may have been having second thoughts. Eleven of the 23 players retained by Derby had refused to accept their new terms: £20 per week, an extra £5 if they were in the first team, and £1 for every 1,000 spectators over 18,000 at home matches. The previous year, the maximum wage for footballers had been abolished. Fulham's Johnny Haynes was reportedly now on £100 a week. In the end, everyone re-signed, but Curry and Swallow were transfer-listed at their own request. They were both still at the Baseball Ground at the start of the following season.

On the morning of the opening match of 1962-63, Reg Matthews reported in with a migraine, so Ken Oxford took his place. Oxford had played only twice since October of the previous season but he stepped up, saved a penalty as the Rams drew 3-3 at Huddersfield, and kept his place for the next 24 games. The new manager had elected to start with the players he inherited but injuries forced him into the transfer market. In September he signed Scotland "B" outside-left Johnny McCann, a player he had developed when he was manager of Barnsley, for £6,000. A month later, Newcastle United left-back Bobby Ferguson joined the Rams for £4,000.

This was going to be an unusual football season. The first snow arrived on Boxing Day and continuous sub-zero temperatures meant that subsequent snowfalls never cleared before the next lot arrived. Easter was in sight before we saw Derby's pavements again. The football season was a major casualty. In one six-week period, almost 500 games were postponed. The Rams played no league games between 22 December and 23 February. Their third-round FA Cup tie against Peterborough United at the Baseball Ground, was postponed six times before Derby won 2-0 in mid-February. Eventually, the FA Cup Final itself had to be delayed. That didn't bother the Rams, however: they had gone out in the fourth round, 3-0 at Leyton Orient. In the Second Division, they spent most of the season in the relegation zone before two wins in their last three games sprung them clear to finish 18th.

In July 1963, Ward went into the transfer market again to bring in Cardiff City's Wales under-23 international inside-left, Alan Durban. Durban cost £10,000 and, although he obviously didn't know it, he would one day share in the greatest days in Derby County's history. Before the season began, Ward dipped into the market again, this time signing Newcastle United's stocky little outside-right, Gordon Hughes, also for £10,000. With Curry dislocating a shoulder it was left to Durban to lead the scorers. That he managed to achieve that without reaching double figures in the league summed up Derby's lack of punch. The Rams finished 13th, much of the credit going to Reg Matthews who had performed brilliantly, week after week.

On 9 September 1964, John Bowers was looking forward to the visit of Coventry City. Five years after making his Rams debut, the part-time footballer – he also worked as a *Derby Evening Telegraph* advertising representative – had at last established himself in the first team. A visit from Jimmy Hill's high-flying Sky Blues was just the stage on which to consolidate his claim. Young John was never going to be as good as his illustrious father. Indeed, he was never going to be the same kind of footballer. Where Jack Bowers dived into a forest of flying boots, John preferred the open space of the wing.

When the teams ran out on the balmy September evening, they found a crowd of 32,803 packed into the Baseball Ground. It was the Rams' biggest attendance since the visit of Grimsby Town for a Third Division North promotion battle, way back in March 1956. After 14 minutes, it was Bowers who put the Rams ahead with the most glorious of goals. Out on the left flank, he pushed the ball inside to Derbyshire cricketer Ian Buxton, and then raced in for the return pass, fighting off two challenges before hammering home a magnificent shot. It should have been his finest hour. But four minutes later he suffered an injury that would keep him out of the game for months. Challenging for the ball, he fell heavily, twisted his ankle and was carried off.

The Rams were now down to 10 men – no substitutes were allowed in league games then – and Coventry, sensing their chance, poured forward. In the Derby goal, however, Matthews was magnificent. After 38 minutes, Bowers – whose famous father was now Derby's physiotherapist – returned, his ankle heavily bandaged, but he was no more than a passenger. Derby, though, held firm and, 19 minutes from the end, they went 2-0 up when Eddie Thomas maintained his record of scoring in every game following his move from Swansea Town two weeks earlier. Even a last-minute goal for Coventry, turned over his own line by Jack Parry, did nothing to spoil the night for the Rams fans that poured out of the Baseball Ground buzzing with what they had just seen.

A week after their fine win, the Rams completed the double over the Sky Blues, winning 2-0 in front of 38,278 spectators at Highfield Road, and after beating Plymouth Argyle 3-2 in the 16th game of the season they were up to third place. Unfortunately, away form let them down and they fell away to finish ninth. They were, however, the Second Division's leading scorers with Durban and Thomas each scoring 22 goals. Towards the end of the season, Colin Boulton took over from the injured Matthews. Boulton came from Ward's hometown of Cheltenham, and had been recommended by his pal, Nigel Cleevely, who had made a scoring debut in a 4-4 draw against Charlton Athletic earlier in the season. Glorious times also lay ahead for the young goalkeeper.

He was not in the team for the start of 1965-66, however. Matthews, fit again, regained his place and kept it all season. But even he couldn't prevent a bad start that saw the Rams collect only four points from their first 10 matches to go bottom of the table. Then Ward introduced three young defenders – John Richardson (Derby's first ever apprentice

Goals galore in this Rams-Blues draw

WHEN Birmingham City visited the Baseball Ground at the end of October 1965, the Rams won an eight-goal thriller, 5-3, with Eddie Thomas and Frank Upton each scoring twice, and Alan Durban providing the other Rams goal.

In the return, on 9 April 1966, Durban was on the mark again, this time as a hat-trick hero in a game that was remarkable from start to finish. Sixteen minutes of the first half alone were truly amazing with five goals in that time.

Birmingham took the lead after 14 minutes, Alec Jackson rounding Mick Hopkinson and Peter Daniel before crossing for the onrushing Trevor Hockey to whip the ball home.

Four minutes later, the Rams were level when Durban dashed in to hammer his shot into the roof of Jim Herriot's net. In the 20th minute, makeshift left-winger Hopkinson played Durban through and the Welshman slid the ball wide of Herriot and watched it roll gently over the line.

Two minutes later, Jackson, cutting in from the right, was tripped by Saxton, and from the penalty spot Malcolm Beard beat Reg Matthews to draw Birmingham level again.

On the half-hour mark, the Blues were 3-2 in front when Jackson fired in a low centre and Saxton, dashing back to cover, diverted the ball into his own net.

Two minutes into the second half, the scoring started all over again. Gordon Hughes beat Birmingham's offside trap with a well-timed pass to Ian Buxton. He cut in from the right and struck a fierce shot just inside the near upright. In the 50th minute, Beard met a Jackson corner and saw his shot go in off the post: 4-3 to Birmingham.

The crowd had to wait a further 20 minutes for another goal, when Geoff Vowden rose to head home Hockey's cross as the Rams defence appealed in vain for offside.

It now seemed that Birmingham had neatly reversed the Baseball Ground scoreline of six months earlier, but ten minutes from time, Hopkinson crashed a loose ball into the goalmouth and the Blues substitute, Bobby Thomson, could only turn it into the net.

Then, with only two minutes remaining, Upton found Buxton and the centre-forward went to the by-line before pulling the ball back to Durban, who completed his hat-trick to make the score 5-5.

In the *Derby Evening Telegraph*, George Edwards reported: "It was just one of those extraordinary games in which both teams forgot about involved defensive systems and got on with the job of trying to score goals ... There was no negative football ... the muddy surface made it difficult for defenders to turn ... and no eight and nine-man defensive barriers ... the odds were on the forwards throughout. If only there were more matches like this one perhaps the grounds would start to fill up again. Unfortunately one sees very few."

professional), Bobby Saxton and Peter Daniel – to play alongside Ron Webster and Frank Upton, who had rejoined the Rams from Chelsea. The reward was instantaneous – only one defeat in the next 16 matches. The Rams improved one place on the previous season's finish, and again the goals had come from Durban (17) and Thomas (13). Buxton, who was still playing first-class cricket, had 12.

In the autumn of 1966, Derby County's players, all dressed in dinner jackets, were guests at the Gaumont on London Road to watch the local premiere of *Goal!*, the official FIFA film of the 1966 World Cup. The Rams themselves had a new goalscorer in their ranks. The season had again begun badly – only one point from their first six matches – and probably no one was more surprised than Tim Ward himself when the board agreed to sign a player that, on the recommendation of chief scout Sammy Crooks, he had been watching for six months. Ward was surprised because his parsimonious directors had agreed to pay a club record transfer fee. And so Bradford Park Avenue's Kevin Hector joined Derby County. Ward recalled: "Eventually I played on chairman Sam Longson's ego. I said, 'Look, Derby could have a record signing – and you could be the chairman who made it possible.' He loved that and agreed to the fee of £34,000. We got Kevin for a lot less than the £40,000 that was bandied about at the time, but it was still a club record."

Kevin Hector made his debut for Derby County at Crystal Palace on 17 September, in a 2-1 defeat in which Billy Hodgson, an outside-left signed from Sheffield United in the summer of 1965, scored the Rams' goal. A week later, Hector made his home debut. The Rams beat Huddersfield Town 4-3 with Durban scoring a hat-trick. But it was Hector's first goal for Derby County that sent the crowd into raptures. In the *Derby Evening Telegraph*, George Edwards summed it up: "They cheered him off the pitch, then they waited half an hour and cheered him out of the ground, jostling to pat him on the back. And no wonder, for nobody could ask more of a player on his debut than Kevin Hector provided at the Baseball Ground on Saturday."

There was still much ground to be made up, and then Hector contracted jaundice ("Do we still have to pay him if he's ill?" one director asked Ward) and Derby had to be satisfied with 17th place. Nevertheless, the fans had already crowned "The King", who finished the season with 16 goals from 30 games.

Tim Ward had certainly found things much more difficult than in his playing days at the Baseball Ground: "I was never really happy as manager, although I probably worked harder at Derby than at any other club. Then in May 1967, Sam Longson said he wanted to see me and I guessed what was coming. He was very embarrassed and just stuttered out that the board had decided not to renew my contract. In many ways it was a relief. I was more disappointed to learn that Ralph Hann, the trainer, and Jack Bowers, his assistant, had also been sacked. Sam asked to see Ralph, who thought that he was going to be asked to stand in until a new manager was appointed. But Sam didn't even ask him into the office. He just told him very curtly in the corridor that he was going as well. It left Ralph in tears."

Ward had signed some fine players, several of whom – Hector, Durban and Boulton in particular – would share in glories still to come. Yet another good signing had stymied his earlier attempts to bring better players to the Baseball Ground: "I got Eddie Thomas for £3,500 from Swansea Town and he scored in his first six games for Derby. After that, the directors expected me to routinely find good players for under £5,000. If I wanted to pay double-figures, I had all sorts of problems. I'd been writing a column for the *Derby Evening Telegraph Football Special* and in my last one, which was just after Derby had sacked me, I said that I'd even had to ask the board for permission to send a letter first class instead of second. It sounded far-fetched, but it was true."

"Brilliant ... that was Cloughie"

THE PROSPECT of a new manager usually improves attendances, for a few weeks at least. So it was no surprise that the Baseball Ground gate for the first match of 1967-68 was an improvement on the previous year. A crowd of 19,412 – some 5,000 up on the opening-day figure 12 months earlier – saw Charlton Athletic beaten 3-2. And as the fans made their way home for tea on that balmy late summer's day of 19 August 1967, they began to think that the new manager might just spring a few surprises. There was also a new centre-forward who, despite looking short of match fitness, had caught their eye. It might be an interesting season.

It was actually a worse season – at least in terms of league position – than the previous campaign. The Rams won the same number of points –36 – but finished one place lower, 18th, than in Tim Ward's final season. For once, however, nobody really minded that a new manager had apparently achieved slightly less than his predecessor. An influx of exciting new players, a run to the semi-finals of the League Cup, and a general feeling that things were getting better, despite what the league table said, all added up.

The Charlton match was the Rams' first under Brian Clough. And the young centre-forward was John O'Hare, signed from Sunderland for £20,000. It may have been an unremarkable start. But it signalled the beginning of the greatest era in Derby County's history. Clough, a goalscoring machine with Middlesbrough and Sunderland before injury halted his playing career, had set Hartlepool United on the road to better things before coming to Derby with his assistant, Peter Taylor, who was already known in the area for his time managing Burton Albion.

In the *Derby Evening Telegraph*, George Edwards commented: "Clearly they were very nervous at the start, particularly new centre-forward O'Hare, who also looked a little short of fitness and therefore mobility. In his case one must obviously reserve judgement and give him time to settle in and it is worth remembering that he rattled in the only chance that came his way without wasting much time ... The poise, calm and complete self-confidence that marks so much of Hector's work was what delighted the fans and it was almost certainly his display as much as anything that sent them home happy."

And happy they were. At the end of the season, few wanted to remind Brian Clough of his pre-season boast that, whatever else happened, the Rams would finish higher than the previous season. Most could see the bigger picture. In the small hours of 26 August 1967, Clough and Taylor completed one of Derby County's best-ever bits of business when they got Tranmere Rovers centre-half, Roy McFarland, out of his bed and wouldn't let him return to his slumber until he had signed for Derby County. The transfer fee was less than £25,000. McFarland's debut came at Rotherham on August Bank Holiday Monday. Derby won 3-1 and George Edwards wrote: "His tackling was fearsomely powerful ... his covering quick and intelligent."

In September, Nottingham Forest's former Wolves and England outside-left, Alan Hinton, arrived at the Baseball Ground, for £30,000. The following month a young full-back from North-East junior football joined the Rams. Despite his lack of experience, John Robson would soon become a key member of the side. Burton Albion centre-forward Richie Barker was almost 28 and had never played in the Football League, but that didn't prevent Clough and Taylor investing in him.

For the League Cup, Clough had to rely on the players that he and Taylor had inherited because the new faces were cup-tied. So men like Phil Waller, Mick Hopkinson, Peter Daniel and Bobby Saxton were regulars in the team that reached the semi-final before losing 4-2 on aggregate to Leeds.

The first leg at the Baseball Ground was watched by almost 30,000 spectators who saw Saxton inexplicably handle the ball to give Leeds a penalty that Johnny Giles converted; it was enough to win the game. It also marked Saxton's last appearance for Derby County. Clough said later: "Sacked him ... he could have headed it." Saxton bore no malice, though: " ... Brilliant. That was Cloughie."

If that tie was a disappointment, however, the following season's League Cup was to bring about one of the greatest nights in Derby County's history. Even supporters who remembered the FA Cup Final triumph of 22 years earlier, agreed. It would surely go down in Rams folklore. It was the night everyone finally realised that something very special was happening at the Baseball Ground. Over the next few years the famous old ground would see plenty of pulsating action, brilliant football and high drama. Nothing, though, would quite compare to the visit of Chelsea in October 1968. The third-round League Cup replay would be the match everyone talked about for years to come. It was the springboard for all the success that followed.

In the close season came the news that Clough had made the audacious signing of Dave Mackay from Tottenham. A football legend would lead the Rams. Yet the season began disappointingly. By 24 August, the Rams had played four league games and failed to win any of them. Then Clough signed Sheffield United's little midfield dynamo, Willie Carlin, for a club record £60,000 fee. Derby lost only three more league games.

Progress in the League Cup had been at the expense of two lower division clubs, Chesterfield and Stockport. The third-round draw sent the Rams to Stamford Bridge where they held Chelsea, third in Division One, to a goalless draw. Cup fever was about to hit Derby.

There were overnight queues for replay tickets, and when York referee, Vic James, got the game under way on a balmy autumn evening, over 34,000 fans packed inside the Baseball Ground. The atmosphere was highly charged, the stage set for a magnificent occasion. The Rams, unbeaten in nine league games and with promotion beginning to seem a possibility, rose to it.

From the kick-off they hammered away at the Chelsea defence, but as the first half wore on it seemed that the Londoners would weather the storm – and might even break away to score against the run of play. That is exactly what happened in the 26th minute. Peter Houseman, who would lose his life so tragically in a car crash, laid on a goal for Alan Birchenall. Birchenall beat Les Green, who had signed from Rochdale in the close season, from fully 30 yards with a brilliant shot into the top corner.

There were only 13 minutes remaining when Derby finally draw level. And what a peach of a goal it was: Carlin impishly backheeled the ball into the path of Mackay who equalised with a dipping 30-yarder.

Seven minutes from the end, Jim Walker robbed Derby-born Ian Hutchinson – who was also to die a tragic and early death – then burst down the left before crossing perfectly for Durban to head past Peter Bonetti. The roar that greeted Durban's goal seemed to rock the Baseball Ground to its very foundations, and four minutes later the ground erupted again. Young full-back John Robson, yet another player from that night who would meet an untimely end, sent over a lovely cross, O'Hare almost turned it in before Hector beat Bonetti to the ball to complete the final act of an epic victory. In the *Derby Evening Telegraph*, George Edwards summed up: "Chelsea went under as wave after wave of white shirts hit them time and again. They were not just outfought – they were outskilled."

In the next round, the Rams repeated the feat, holding Everton, the previous season's FA Cup Finalists, to a goalless draw before beating them in front of another 34,000 crowd at the Baseball Ground. The Rams' run ended in anticlimax, though, when they lost 1-0 in a replay at Third Division Swindon.

At the end of November, after winning at Crystal Palace, Derby went to the top of the table, and they did not relinquish that. On 29 March, the Rams travelled to Villa Park where the home manager, Tommy Docherty, promised them "no more than a cup of tea". Dave Simmons, under pressure from O'Hare, turned a McFarland effort over his own line for the only goal of the game, and 8,000 Derby supporters in the 49,000 crowd sang: "Tommy put the kettle on." On the final day of the season over 31,000 fans greeted the Second Division champions when they ran out to play Bristol City at the Baseball Ground. Dave Mackay accepted the trophy, Alan Durban scored a hat-trick, and the Rams won 5-0. It was the perfect end to a brilliant season. Bringing Mackay had been an inspired move, but the signing of Carlin had been key. The influence that he wielded on the pitch was immense. Midfielders Jim Walker and John McGovern, both Clough-Taylor signings, played their part, as did former England forward Frank Wignall, who came as late-season cover from Wolves. Hector topped the scorers with 16 goals. The question was: could he do it in the First Division? We were about to find out.

Not So Much a Match as a Massacre

Derby County fans poured out of the Baseball Ground on 20 September 1969, hardly able to believe what they had just seen. In only their 11th game back in the top flight, Derby had beaten Tottenham Hotspur, Jimmy

Greaves and all. No, more than that, they hadn't just beaten the Londoners – they had outplayed them, thrashed them, humiliated them. And they had done it before the biggest crowd ever to watch a Rams home game. In the *Derby Evening Telegraph* George Edwards summed it up perfectly: "It wasn't a match, it was a massacre."

The Rams had made a memorable start to their first season in the First Division for 16 years. By the time Tottenham arrived, Brian Clough's team still had to taste defeat, and looked to extend a winning run to five games. They managed it with something to spare. The Tottenham team that contained so many famous names – Greaves, Pat Jennings, Alan Mullery, Mike England, Alan Gilzean and the rest – boasted a pedigree that had no answer to the onslaught unleashed by Derby on that balmy early autumn afternoon. The Rams hit five goals without reply in front of a record crowd of 41,826. Many of them sat in the new Ley Stand that in the close season had risen above the Popular Side. Wrote Edwards: "Sustained brilliance with a dash of sheer cruelty enabled Derby County to reduce Spurs to an inept shambles of a team ... At times it was simply not a fair contest. Jimmy Greaves and Co were just not capable of giving the Rams a decent game."

Durban (two), Carlin, O'Hare and Hector scored in a victory was all the more remarkable for the fact that Tottenham had arrived at the Baseball Ground with the best away record in the First Division and had won their previous four away games. When Tottenham manager, Bill Nicholson, asked: "Was Dave Mackay playing today?" he was simply underlining the fact that the Rams had had no need of the former Spurs star's abilities as a sweeper. Nicholson told post-match press conference: "They humiliated us ... Their midfield players were great. Carlin? How big is he? Four foot nine? Brilliant ... You can watch Spurs play for the next five years and you won't see Mike England be made to struggle like that again. Dave Mackay? If I wanted all this to happen for anybody it would be him. Six Dave Mackays and you wouldn't need anybody else ... One of the all-time greats."

At the final whistle John McGovern dashed over to Greaves, explaining later: "He's such a great player. I just wanted to shake his hand." Which neatly summed up the measure of Derby's epic achievement.

Derby County had made a storming start to life back at the top, and when Manchester United arrived in early October, another 40,000-plus Baseball Ground crowd saw United beaten 2-0. The Rams had a little

Gunners spiked as the Rams hit top form

WHEN Arsenal arrived at the Baseball Ground on 21 February 1970, Derby County embarked upon an unbeaten run that would take them to the fringes of the title race.

True, Arsenal themselves might have scored a couple more in what turned out to be a 3-2 victory for the Rams, but as George Edwards commented in the *Derby Evening Telegraph*: "...in one 30-minute purple patch, the Rams could have approached double figures and still missed a few."

The Rams had entered 1970 in contention for the title, and on 11 February, the day Terry Hennessey made his debut following his £100,000 transfer from Forest, they drew 2-2 at home to Chelsea. It was the start of a remarkable run that would see the Rams go through the rest of the season unbeaten.

The visit of Arsenal was the third game in that 12-match run, yet it was a match the Rams had to "win twice" after falling behind.

Indeed, early on Arsenal looked capable of winning almost as easily as their 4-0 victory at Highbury back in November, and it was no great surprise when they went in front after 13 minutes, John Radford's volley beating a bemused Les Green, who might have been unsighted.

But if it was a mistake, it was not as bad as the one by the inexperienced John Roberts that enabled Kevin Hector to score a brilliant equaliser seven minutes later. Roberts, a former railway fireman, tried to turn the ball back to Bob Wilson but mishit it and Hector, darting in quickly, drove a terrific shot just inside the far post from what looked like an impossible angle.

After 35 minutes, the Gunners were back in front when their first corner of the match eluded Green, Bob McNab forced the ball back across goal, and Roberts made amends by turning it into the Derby net.

The Rams laboured unconvincingly until the interval. But whatever Brian Clough and Peter Taylor said to the players at half-time, it certainly had the required effect.

George Edwards described what happened next: "Almost from the kick-off, Hinton crossed from the left, Hector headed the ball down beautifully, and O'Hare, in an almost unbelievably huge space, took it on and toe-ended it past Wilson.

"A minute later came the winner – another odd goal for which Wilson, otherwise highly convincing in the air, must take most of the responsibility. When Mackay lofted in an angled centre, Carlin ran in and tried to head the ball. Wilson took his eye off it and it curled gently into the net despite the effort of Storey to keep it out.

"... Further goals, however, would not come, and Arsenal occasionally broke menacingly ... but the Rams rocked and finally wrecked Arsenal with a tremendous comeback highlighted by brilliant displays by John O'Hare and Kevin Hector." And 35,000 Rams fans went home happy.

New Year wobble but six wins on the bounce in February and March – Arsenal, Liverpool, Manchester City and Forest were among the names to fall – settled things down again. In February, Derby County broke their transfer record again, paying £100,000 for Welsh international Terry Hennessey, who was lined up to replace the veteran Mackay, although Mackay showed no signs of wanting to give up his place in the team. The most surprising thing about the Hennessey transfer was that Nottingham Forest agreed to let him go to Derby in the first place.

A 4-0 hammering of Leeds United on Easter Monday had a hollow ring because Leeds, in a bid to spare their first-team as they chased a European Cup and FA Cup double, fielded their entire reserve side. In the *Derby Evening Telegraph*, George Edwards summed up the mood: " … the crowd was so big that the gates were locked 20 minutes before the kick-off – but that was probably to stop them getting out when the teams were announced." Their decision to field a weakened team cost Leeds a £5,000 Football League fine, and helped the Rams on the way to taking 20 points from the final 24 available to finish in fourth place and qualify for the UEFA Cup. European football so soon – for Rams fans it seemed like a dream. And it may as well have been. A joint FA-Football League enquiry found the Rams administration guilty of "gross negligence", and fined the club £10,000. Worse, Derby County were banned from European competition for one year. Derby's mayor, Tom Taylor, called it "a terrible injustice". Supporters didn't know what to think.

They didn't know what to think in February 1971, either, when they bought their *Evening Telegraph* and read that the Rams had broken the British transfer record for a defender in order to bring Sunderland's Colin Todd to the Baseball Ground. It wasn't the biggest new local news story of that month, however. On 4 February, Roll-Royce, the town's biggest employer, had gone bust. It was unthinkable: the very epitome of perfection in British engineering had collapsed. Roll-Royce had been brought down by the escalating development costs of the RB211 engine. Thousands of those affected at the time – because they were either employed by Roll-Royce or worked for companies that depended on contracts with R-R – were Rams supporters. And football was their escape. As J. B. Priestley wrote in *The Good Companions*, the game helped them escape "from the clanking machinery of this lesser life, from work, wages, rent, dole, sick pay, insurance cards … " And there was plenty of escapism to be found at the Baseball Ground. Before he astonished the rest of football by paying such a large fee for Todd, Brian Clough had already made one major dip into the transfer market that season when, in September 1970, he paid £50,000 for Preston's Scotland under-23 midfielder, Archie Gemmill. That allowed him to sell Willie Carlin to Leicester City, for £40,000, although Carlin was adamant that he didn't want to leave Derby.

By November, the Rams were a dangerous 19th in the table, which underlined Clough's warning after the players had supped champagne following the pre-season Watney Cup Final victory over Manchester United, "when we hadn't played even one real match". For parts of the season the Rams lost McFarland and Hennessey to injuries, and Les Green played his last game for the Rams, in a 4-4 Boxing Day draw against Manchester United at the Baseball Ground. He gave way to Colin Boulton who embarked upon a record-breaking run.

McFarland, in particular, recovered to play brilliantly and five successive wins in January and February took Derby up to the middle of the table before four defeats in five games dropped them back down to 14th. After that, the Rams lost only once more, however, to finish ninth.

Champions of England

The majority of the 39,159 crowd who packed into the Baseball Ground on the warm, pleasant evening of 1 May 1972 were setting their sights on a UEFA Cup place – provided the game's rulers didn't step in again and snatch the prize of European football from them. Derby County stood third in the First Division with 56 points from 41 matches, behind Manchester City (57 points from a completed programme) and Liverpool (56 from 40). Immediately below the Rams were Leeds United with 55 points and, like the Merseysiders, with two games left. Too many bits of the jigsaw had to fall into place for Derby fans to think about their club winning the Football League championship for the first time in its history.

Dave Mackay had moved to Swindon Town as player-manager, Les Green had gone to South African soccer, John Richardson was transferred to Notts County, and the Rams began 1971-72 with a very small first-team squad. None the less, at the beginning of March, with 40 points from 30 matches, they stood third in the table. Manchester City had opened up a five-point gap with Leeds in second place, a point ahead of Derby. By then the Rams were in the middle of an epic FA Cup battle against Arsenal, a fifth-round tie that was watched, in total, by 143,000 spectators. The game at Derby was drawn 2-2, thanks to an

88th-minute goal from Alan Durban. The replay attracted over 63,000 to Highbury, a staggering attendance considering that the match was played on a Wednesday afternoon because power restrictions ruled out the use of floodlights. A goalless draw saw the sides move to neutral territory – Filbert Street – where 40,000 saw John McGovern try a 30-yard back-pass that cannoned off Todd, allowing Ray Kennedy to deny the Rams their first appearance in the quarter-finals of the FA Cup for 22 years. Nine days earlier, Derby had introduced Ian Storey-Moore to Baseball Ground fans as the Rams' latest signing. Nottingham Forest had other ideas, however, and Storey-Moore eventually went to Old Trafford, while an embarrassed Derby County were fined for jumping the gun.

On Easter Saturday, the Rams were still in second place when they entertained Leeds. Both sides had 49 points from 35 matches – Manchester City were still top with 50 points from 35 games – and the Rams took Leeds apart in beating them 2-0. The margin could have been much greater than the goals from O'Hare and Norman Hunter, who, much to the delight of Derby fans, put the ball into his own net.

The Leeds game took its toll and on Easter Monday, Newcastle won 1-0 at the Baseball Ground. McFarland was off the field a while having five stitches inserted in a head wound, and Boulton was nursing a fractured finger sustained five weeks previously. Two days later the Rams drew 0-0 at The Hawthorns, then hammered Sheffield United 4-0 at Bramall Lane. That took Derby to 54 points, their highest-ever total from a First Division season – and there were still three matches remaining. Hector scored his 200th League goal at Bramall Lane, and when Huddersfield were beaten 3-0 at the Baseball Ground a week later, the Rams were the bookmakers' favourites for the title.

However, on the last Saturday of the First Division season the picture again changed dramatically. Derby lost 2-0 at Maine Road – City's last fixture – while Leeds beat West Brom 1-0, and Liverpool beat Ipswich 2-0. The Rams had only one league match remaining, but before that they had to play their postponed Texaco Cup Final second leg. On 26 April, Derby beat Airdrie 2-1 in a niggly game that saw Drew Jarvie on the wrong end of a Colin Boulton punch. Referee Jack Taylor contented himself with a quiet word, but after the incident was replayed on television the Rams fined their goalkeeper.

Then it was time to meet Liverpool. An evenly matched game was 63 minutes old when Archie Gemmill speared a ball into the penalty area,

Alan Durban jumped over it, and John McGovern, falling, hit his shot high into the roof of Ray Clemence's net. It was enough to win the game. There were 11 heroes in this victory that put the Rams back at the top of the First Division, but none more heroic than 16-year-old Steve Powell. In what was only his second full league game, Powell played with a maturity way beyond his years. "I wasn't nervous," he said. "I just wanted to get out and play."

The same evening, however, Leeds beat Chelsea 2-0 at Elland Road, and even after the Rams' superb victory over the Merseysiders, it still appeared that either or both Liverpool and Leeds would overhaul Derby who now stood head of the First Division. Thus, Derby County went on their post-season break with a UEFA Cup place already assured. On Monday, 8 May 1972, as the Rams players enjoyed a leisurely evening meal in Majorca, Liverpool travelled to Arsenal, while Leeds, in search of a Football League and FA Cup double, went to Molineux. Leeds lost 2-1. Liverpool could only draw at Highbury. All of which meant that Derby County were champions of England.

European Nights

When Real Madrid were embarking on their fantastic run of European Cup successes in the mid-1950s, Derby County's Third Division North fixture list comprised the likes of Gateshead, Southport and Workington. So it was with feelings of awe and disbelief that Rams supporters considered the fact that the names of Real Madrid *and* Derby County were going into the draw for the 1972-73 European Cup. Competitive European football – if you discount the April 1962 Friendship Cup match against the French club, AS Béziers – came to the Baseball Ground for the first time on 13 September 1972 when the Yugoslavian champions, FK Zeljeznicar (the name means "railway worker") of Sarajevo, were beaten 2-0 by goals from McFarland and Gemmill. John Robson, who had missed only one league game in the championship-winning season, played that night, although he had lost his regular left-back place to David Nish, an elegant defender signed from Leicester City for £225,000 just two weeks into the new season. Nish had arrived too late to be eligible for the early European rounds and so Robson stepped back up. There were 27,500 spectators at the Baseball Ground that evening, and 60,000 in Zeljeznicar's Kosevo Stadium to see Derby complete their task with a 2-1 win, this time Hinton and O'Hare scoring for the Rams.

The second round saw a brief reunion between Derby County and one of their pre-war players. Portuguese champions, Benfica, were managed by Jimmy Hagan, one of the greatest talents ever to escape the Baseball Ground after George Jobey sold him to Sheffield United for £2,500 back in November 1938. In October 1972 his "Eagles of Lisbon" must have wondered where they had landed as their team coach threaded its way through the tight, terraced streets around the Baseball Ground. They must have been equally taken aback when they wandered out for a first look at the pitch and found it waterlogged in early November. Even FA secretary, Sir Stanley Rous, was puzzled. "It hasn't been raining in London," he told Brian Clough, who just shrugged. "I'd been up all night, watering it," whispered Clough, confidentially, years later, although it wasn't much of a secret at the time. After only 30 minutes on that soggy surface, the Rams stormed into a 3-0 lead – McFarland, Hector and McGovern – and it turned into a night to rival that great Chelsea League Cup-tie of five years earlier. Benfica were torn to shreds and a 20-second floodlit failure at the Estadio da Luz – Stadium of Light – could not help them, even though the great Eusebio was bearing down on Colin Boulton at the time. When the lights went on again, the Rams goalkeeper was relieved to see that an equally surprised Eusebio had let the ball escape him for a goal-kick and the scoreline was still 0-0 when the final whistle sounded.

Nish was now eligible to play for the Rams in Europe, and Robson was therefore sold to Aston Villa for a Derby record incoming fee of £90,000. Robson would help Villa win promotion to the First Division and lift the League Cup twice before his career was ended by multiple sclerosis, from which he died in May 2004, aged 53. Nish took his place for the quarter-final tie against Spartak Trnava, and although the Rams won 1-0 in Czechoslovakia and 2-1 at the Baseball Ground, it was a nervous ending because another away goal for the Czechs would have put them through.

Was there no limit to the footballing miracles that Brian Clough and Peter Taylor could perform? Derby County were into the semi-final of the European Cup where they faced the Italian giants, Juventus. Ahead of the first leg in Turin, Clough and Taylor travelled to see Juventus in a Serie A game. After the first leg, Taylor told the players, "We daren't tell you what they were like. They played just like a Third Division side." Sure enough, in Turin the Rams were level at 1-1 at half-time. Hector's goal – the first ever scored by an English club in a European Cup match in Italy

– had levelled Altafini's effort of two minutes earlier. Causio and Altafini again scored to give Juventus a 3-1 win, but there were some funny goings-on, McFarland and Gemmill were booked for trivial offences by West German referee, Gerhard Schulenburg, and they missed the second leg. There was a half-time bust-up in the tunnel when Peter Taylor tried to follow the German referee, who was deep in conversation with his fellow countryman, the Juventus player Helmut Haller. Former Wales international John Charles, who had played for Juventus and was a hugely popular figure in Turin, had travelled with Derby as an advisor. He told Taylor that Haller was in the referee's dressing room. Taylor tried to intervene and was arrested, although he was soon released when Charles stepped in. The situation wasn't helped when Clough insisted that his post-match words for the Italian press were translated literally: "I will not speak to cheating bastards."

At Derby the Rams failed to break down a massed Italian defence. Even when Spinosi tripped Hector, Hinton sent the penalty wide. Centre-forward Roger Davies, who had joined the Rams from non-League Worcester City in September 1971 for £12,000, was sent off for reacting wildly to a piece of provocation. The goalless draw put the Rams out. There were more dark mutterings, including a rumour that someone had approached the Portuguese referee, Francisco Marques Lobo, and offered him a bribe to help Juventus win. In fact, a notorious fixer, allegedly on behalf of the Juventus club, had indeed contacted Lobo. The referee was offered a car, $5,000, and the promise that Dr Artemio Franchi, president of both Juventus and the Italian Football Federation, would "promote his career" as an international referee. But the honourable Lobo had refused and immediately reported the matter to UEFA who, after hearing the evidence, decided to let him officiate at the Baseball Ground. No action was taken against Juventus or Franchi because no connection between them and the shady fixer could be proved. Franchi was soon to become president of UEFA. Interestingly, the Derby-Juventus game was the last European match that Lobo would ever referee.

In the First Division, the Rams away form let them down badly and they lost 12 matches on opponents' grounds to finish seventh. Leeds won 1-0 at Derby in the sixth round of the FA Cup, but the real excitement had come in the fourth round. Nearly 38,000 saw Spurs draw 1-1 at the Baseball Ground, and there were nearly 53,000 present for the replay when the Londoners led 3-1 with 10 minutes remaining. But the Rams fought back magnificently and won 5-3 in extra-time, thanks to two goals from Hector and a brilliant hat-trick from Davies which earned the Rams one of the greatest come-backs in the history of the FA Cup.

"We've Had Enough Of Crawling"

On 13 October 1973, Kevin Hector's goal at Old Trafford earned Derby County a 1-0 win and third place in the First Division. A week later the Rams entertained Leicester City at the Baseball Ground. In between came a series of events that became more bizarre with each passing hour. It was no secret that Brian Clough had been at loggerheads with the Derby directors – and in particular with chairman Sam Longson, the man who said he carried a picture of Clough in his wallet and wanted to adopt him – mainly over the manager's television appearances and brushes with the game's authorities. Even so, the events that followed the win against United staggered football.

Mrs Clough and Mrs Taylor had been to Old Trafford as guests of Manchester United because no tickets had been made available to them in the visiting directors' box. And when Clough and Taylor returned to the Baseball Ground that evening to toast a fine win, they found that the bar in the manager's office, used to provide hospitality to visitors, had been cleared. Storm clouds that had gathered over the Baseball Ground in the preceding months were about to break with a ferocity never before seen in football. Two days later Clough and Taylor were working on a newspaper article when they were handed a letter from Longson, a letter that, in effect, was an ultimatum over Clough's TV work. Clough's reaction was fairly predictable. He rang Longson and asked for a special board meeting that night to tender their resignations. Longson refused, saying that he did not want to drive back from his North Derbyshire home that evening, and that Clough must put his resignation in writing. This they did, asking *Derby Evening Telegraph* sportswriter Gerald Mortimer to type out the letters because they didn't wish to embarrass their secretary.

Thus on Tuesday, 16 October, press, radio and television descended on the Baseball Ground and the very thing about which the Derby directors were so sensitive – the glare of publicity – suddenly burst upon them with remorseless searching. The board met quickly and announced that the resignations had been accepted, although one director, Mike Keeling, had resigned in protest. There followed an undignified press conference with both sides holding court in the same room. It was all very embarrassing and the sad affair ended with Longson being prised away by another director, Jack Kirkland.

Clough told the *Derby Evening Telegraph*: "My knees and elbows are sore from all the crawling that Peter and I have had to do these last few months. Only two things have kept us here for so long. First and foremost, the players. Secondly, the supporters. They haven't always agreed with us but they've always gone along with what we've tried to do. Before the Sunderland game last week, while we were talking to the chairman, other directors were going through our contracts. They were looking for ways in which they could find us at fault."

The Derby players were as shell-shocked as the fans. Four of them, McFarland, Todd, Nish and Hector, were away training with England for the forthcoming World Cup qualifier against Poland at Wembley. The rest decided to await their return before deciding what to do. Jimmy Gordon, the first-team trainer, took charge and reminded the players that they had to set about beating Leicester four days later, to stay on target for the title. The Leicester game was won 2-1 but it will be remembered less for the football than for the amazing scenes that preceded it. The sight of Longson, in the directors' box, and Clough from an adjoining stand, greeted the players. The two men vied for the support of a 32,000 crowd. Clough had arrived in a Rolls-Royce minutes earlier, and both men stood waving to the crowd, Longson apparently thinking that the cheers for Clough were in fact intended for him. After a few minutes, Clough left the ground to appear on Michael Parkinson's TV chat show.

Seven days after the two had resigned, Roy McFarland handed the board a letter. It read: "During the events of the last week we, the undersigned players, have kept our feelings within the dressing-room. However, at this time we are unanimous in our support for Mr Clough and Mr Taylor and ask that they be reinstated as manager and assistant manager of this club. It was absolutely vital that we won on Saturday, both for ourselves as well as for the club and the fans. Now that match is out of the way, nobody can say that we have acted on the spur of the moment or are just being emotional."

The letter was signed by all the first-team squad with the exception of Henry Newton, Derby's £100,000 signing from Everton, who was away in Liverpool on business. It was handed to Longson as the Derby board were trying to entice Bobby Robson to leave Ipswich Town. The players asked Clough and Taylor to meet them at the Kedleston Hotel where they showed them a copy of the letter sent to the board. Clough asked the players to take their wives and children to the Newton Park Hotel, near Burton, that evening. When they arrived, the former manager ordered 30 bottles of champagne – and the players noticed journalists and TV cameras in the hotel foyer. Clough and Taylor and the players went into a private room and it was there that a staggering suggestion was made – that the players should fly out of the country, perhaps to Spain, so that they could not play for the Rams that Saturday. It was an outrageous idea because the players would have been in serious breach of their contracts.

While Clough, Taylor and the players sat and talked, Derby's directors were in Nottingham, setting up the deal which would bring Nottingham Forest manager Dave Mackay back to Derby, although the signing would not be announced until after Forest's match against Hull City the following evening. Next morning, London solicitors acting for Clough issued a High Court writ against Derby County and five directors, alleging libel "in a written statement published on or about 18 October".

Meanwhile, the players met at the home of Archie Gemmill and, in the absence of a reply to their letter, they each in turn telephoned the Baseball Ground and asked to speak to a director. Each time they were refused until an official at the ground said that all the members of the board had left. Undaunted, the Rams players got into three cars and went to the Baseball Ground. What they saw confirmed their suspicions. Jack Kirkland's Mercedes was parked outside the directors' entrance and in the boardroom a light was burning. For four hours the players laid siege to the Baseball Ground in one of the most amazing episodes in the history of any football club. Eventually Kirkland and secretary Stuart Webb emerged from a darkened boardroom with the players just down the corridor, and sped off to Nottingham's Albany Hotel to sign Mackay. Webb later told how the directors had been so desperate not to leave the boardroom that an ice-bucket had been pressed into service as a makeshift urinal.

Back at Gemmill's house, Roy McFarland put through a call to the City Ground where Forest's Bill Anderson told him that Mackay was at that moment meeting Derby officials at the Albany Hotel. Eventually, McFarland was able to contact Mackay – no mobile phones in those days – and in a long telephone conversation told him that it would be unwise of him to accept the Derby job because of the feeling of the players for Clough and Taylor. Mackay had only one answer: he could not possibly turn down a contract that the newspapers later reported was in the region of £20,000 a year.

The Rams players then spoke on the telephone to each of the Derby directors in turn – "in a heated and uncomplimentary manner", according to Colin Boulton – but to no avail. Boulton, one of the leaders of the players' bring-back-Clough campaign, said: "We met Mackay the following day and none of us said much, except Roy Mac, who explained the players' feelings. Mackay told us that he knew how we must feel and that if he had still been a player at Derby, then he would have been the first to sign our letter. But he was now the boss and would not tolerate any upheavals. One month after our meeting with Clough and Taylor, we formulated a letter that said we were dissatisfied with Dave Mackay and his assistant, Des Anderson. We said that we wanted Cloughie and Taylor reinstated immediately and that we would train on our own on a local park before the next game, against Leeds. By this time, morale was low and we'd slipped to eighth in the table. But the letter went undelivered because the PFA warned that we would be in breach of contract."

Clough and Taylor had one more meeting with the players, at the Midland Hotel where the Rams footballers told the former Derby managerial team that there was nothing more they could do, even allowing for the overwhelming public support for the two. The players said their goodbyes and both Clough and Taylor were visibly shaken at the emotion of the meeting.

After beating Leicester "for Brian and Peter", Derby went six games without a win, suffered three successive defeats and by the beginning of December had dropped to ninth. But even amidst all the drama, the Rams were still a talented side – chairman Sam Longson had announced, "Even I could manage this lot!" – and slowly their class began to tell. In the first 13 league matches of 1974, Derby lost only once. In February, Mackay, looking for more scoring power from midfield, paid Aston Villa £200,00 for Bruce Rioch. Seventeen points from a possible 26 lifted Derby back among the leaders. Three wins out of the last four matches took them to third place, a massive 14 points behind champions, Leeds, and nine points adrift of runners-up, Liverpool. Dave Mackay had steadied an unstable ship. But the presence of Brian Clough would overshadow successive Derby County managers for some time to come.

Mackay's Champions

I N MAY 1974, Roy McFarland was playing in the opening game of the Home International Championship at Ninian Park when he felt a slight twinge in the Achilles' tendon of his left leg. Four days later, against Northern Ireland at Wembley, McFarland fell heavily when challenging Sammy Morgan and was carried off with a severed tendon. It was 11 months before he played in the First Division again. The Rams faced almost an entire season without their England centre-half.

Dave Mackay did not sign a replacement, however (in fact the only addition to the Rams squad was the former England striker, Francis Lee, who came from Manchester City three days before the season began, for £100,000). Instead, he relied upon a defender who had been on Derby's books since Tim Ward's day. Peter Daniel hadn't managed even one appearance when the Rams won the Football League championship in 1971-72, and he'd played only eight times in 1972-73, although when McFarland was suspended for the home leg of the European Cup semi-final, he had stepped in and performed superbly against Juventus. But with the only other option, Welsh international Rod Thomas, injured in a pre-season game, Daniel played at centre-half in the opening match of 1973-74 – a goalless draw at Everton – and he kept his place for the rest of the season. It was as if the description "unsung hero" had been coined especially for him.

The Rams won only one of their first seven league matches, by which time the first round of the UEFA Cup was almost upon them. Derby's second venture into Europe began quietly enough when the Swiss side, Servette, were beaten 6-2 on aggregate. Less than 18,000 turned up to watch the first leg at the Baseball Ground. It was a different tale in the second round, however, when over 29,000 came streaming through the darkened streets to see one of the most famous names in football – Atlético Madrid, the previous season's European Cup Finalists. The Spaniards had a reputation other than for fine football. In their European Cup semi-final, a brutal match against Celtic at Parkhead had seen three Madrid players sent off and another four booked. Their manager, Juan Carlos Lorenzo, was in charge of the 1966 Argentina side dubbed "animals" by Sir Alf Ramsey, and also of the notorious Italian club, Lazio, whose players had attacked Arsenal players outside a Rome restaurant in 1970.

In the first leg at the Baseball Ground the Rams were held 2-2. After Ayala had shot Atlético ahead, Nish levelled the scores. Then the French referee gave two highly dubious penalties. First Boulton was penalised for grabbing the ball from the feet of Garate and the Spaniards went ahead again from the spot; then Lee fell dramatically in the area and with the referee perhaps thinking that he ought to even things up, Rioch stepped forward to slam home the equaliser. In the Vicente Calderón Stadium, the Rams knew that they must avoid conceding an early goal, but after only four minutes Luis rose unchallenged to head home Adelardo's cross. Gradually Derby settled down and Rioch and Hector made it 2-1 before Luis scored his second with an overhead kick. After 30 minutes extra-time, the aggregate was still 4-4 and the game hinged on a penalty decider. The scores were still level when Eusebio stepped up to take the 16th kick. Boulton guessed correctly, parried the ball with his left hand and although Eusebio followed up to smash the rebound into the net, it did not matter.

In the third round Derby faced a little-known Yugoslavian side, Velez Mostar, and on a cloying Baseball Ground pitch won the first leg 3-1, thanks to two inspired substitutions. Velez went ahead after only three minutes and Derby could not get back into the game until Jeff Bourne and Alan Hinton came on. First Bourne, a Clough signing from Linton United in 1969, turned home Hector's centre. Then Hinton put Derby ahead with a brilliant goal. With three minutes remaining, Bourne made it 3-1. It was tremendous fight-back, but in the misty glare of the Gradski Stadium, the Rams disintegrated. Primorac netted after Gemmill conceded a penalty, and then Pecelj levelled the aggregate. As firecrackers shot across the pitch, Valdic made it 3-0 on the night, and although Hector levelled the aggregate score, Velez found the winner from a controversial penalty. Todd was unable to avoid a fierce close-range shot from Hadziabdic that smashed against his forearm. Dutch referee Charles Corver pointed to the spot and Bajevic rammed home Velez's second spot-kick of the match. Derby protested to UEFA about the referee and the crowd, but although the Rams appeared in the draw for the next round, Velez went through after being fined a paltry £500.

When the Rams picked up the league programme, tiredness showed. The only consolation was that the leadership was constantly changing hands, and by New Year's Eve, the Rams were three points from the top of the table. On 22 February, Steve Powell's goals gave Derby a 2-1 win over Arsenal, as Alan Ball and Bob McNab were sent off at the Baseball Ground. But consistency still eluded the Rams and seven days later they lost 3-0 at Portman Road. Lee, whose goal touch had deserted him, was injured and Hinton came into the team. Together with Davies he added a new dimension to the Rams' game and they began their run-in for the title with 19 points from 12 games. On 15 March, a 2-1 home defeat by Stoke left Derby now desperately needing to win at Newcastle. Their previous season's victory at St James's Park had been their first under Mackay. This one was even more vital, and Nish and Rioch scored the goals that gave Derby a 2-0 win.

Easter Saturday 1975 was a game that one Rams player would never forget, as Gerald Mortimer told *Derby Evening Telegraph* readers: "Roger Davies humiliated and destroyed Luton Town's defence at the Baseball Ground on Saturday. He scored all Derby County's five goals, had two more disallowed and saw a ferocious shot finely saved by Keith Barber ..."

On Easter Monday, Burnley were thrashed 5-2 at Turf Moor, and the following evening, Manchester City went down to two Rioch goals at the Baseball Ground to give the Rams six points out of six over Easter.

A touch of good fortune earned the Rams a draw at Middlesbrough when Hector took advantage of Stuart Boam's slip, and then Roy McFarland made his return against Wolves when Peter Daniel – who was about to be voted that season's player of the year by supporters – moved to left-back in place of the injured Nish. Lee also returned and glanced in a Gemmill corner to give Derby a 1-0 win. The Rams moved to the top of the table, and unlike 1972, could now win the title without waiting for other teams to fail. West Ham were beaten 1-0, but Derby could not finish the season on an emphatic note, drawing their last two games, at Leicester, and at home to Carlisle, when 180 minutes' football failed to produce a goal. Before the Carlisle game the Rams said hello to a parade of former stars. Afterwards they said goodbye to the infamous Baseball Ground pitch. It was a testament to the players signed by Clough and Taylor, and by Mackay, that such magnificent football had been played for so long on what was so often six inches deep in cloying mud. Now it was to be dug up and replaced.

For the second time Derby County were crowned champions while sitting in a nightspot. They were celebrating the club's annual awards night at Bailey's club in Colyear Street when news came through that Ipswich had dropped a point to Manchester City, which meant that the Rams could not be overtaken even though their 53 points was the lowest total by a championship-winning side since Chelsea's 52 in 1955.

A Last Hurrah

On 9 August 1975, in the FA Charity Shield game at Wembley, Derby County faced West Ham United, 2-0 FA Cup Final winners over Fulham the previous May. There were 59,000 shirt-sleeved fans to see the Rams win 2-0 with goals from Kevin Hector and Roy McFarland. Making a promising debut for Derby that afternoon was Charlie George, signed for £90,000 from Arsenal the previous month. George might have made the almost unthinkable switch from Highbury to White Hart Lane but Dave Mackay heard that the striker was available and interrupted his holiday in Scotland to fly to London to arrange the deal that would bring one of the game's most colourful players to Derby.

The Rams' defence of their championship got off to a bad start. After two away draws they were run ragged at the Baseball Ground where Stan Bowles scored a hat-trick in QPR's 5-1 win. By the end of August, the Rams had won only once and were 19th in the First Division. Defeat at Everton three days later did nothing to ease matters, but then four consecutive wins – against Burnley, Spurs, Manchester City and Manchester United – were enough to send the champions soaring up the table to sixth place. Boulton, who had injured an ankle in a League Cup win at Huddersfield, had to stand down for the game at White Hart Lane. It was only the third match that Boulton had missed out of 253, the others the result of a suspension after the goalkeeper argued with Tonbridge referee Ron Challis following a match against Leeds at Derby in April 1973.

Boulton's injury improved sufficiently for Mackay to recall him for the European Cup first-round, first-leg match against Slovan Bratislava at the compact Tehelné Pole stadium, across the river from Trnava where, two years earlier, the Rams had played a European Cup quarter-final match against Slovan's fierce rivals. Hector missed the match because of a one-match European suspension. Rioch hit the base of an upright and, five minutes into the second half, George was well clear but squandered the opportunity, leaving a fluke goal by Marian Masny to divide the teams at the final whistle. From a corner the ball hit the back of Masny's head and flew past Boulton, who was already going the other way.

Not surprisingly, the Czechs brought a massed defence to the Baseball Ground, yet it was an incident that might have had disastrous consequences for the Rams that finally led to Derby breaking through. Newton twisted his ankle and was replaced by Jeff Bourne, who had been on the transfer list for some time. On the stroke of half-time Bourne curled a shot past Vencel and in off a post. In the second half, Nish hit the woodwork. Then, with 12 minutes remaining, Lee hammered home a brilliant goal from Todd's pass. Two minutes later, Lee was hanging his head in despair after missing a penalty, but he need not have worried. Two minutes after that, after a shot from Nish was blocked, he was on hand to pick up a rebound and make the aggregate 3-1.

Derby County would now meet the greatest name in European soccer, Real Madrid. And after only 10 minutes of the first leg at the Baseball Ground, the Rams took the lead with a breathtaking goal. Todd hit a magnificent pass out to Nish on the far side of the field and he slipped it through to Archie Gemmill. Gemmill's shot fizzed across the face of the Real goal and Charlie George screamed in to give Angel no chance with a fierce left-footer. Seven minutes later, the Rams were two ahead. Lee was sent sprawling and George hit home his first penalty for Derby. Pirri pulled one back for Real, and the Rams needed another goal. It arrived shortly before half-time: McFarland took the ball deep into the Real half before laying a pass to Nish, who hit a rasping shot just under the bar. In the second half, Angel made brilliant saves from Rioch and Lee; and when Pirri found the Derby net again, the Soviet linesman Tofiq Bahramov – the man who decided that Geoff Hurst's shot in the 1966 World Cup Final was over the line – flagged for offside. Real's protests came to nothing. The Spaniards protested even more bitterly in the 78th minute when Netzer pulled down Hector and George completed his hat-trick from the spot. Derby 4, Real Madrid 1. Few in the 35,000 Baseball Ground crowd could quite believe it.

Just as in Madrid a year earlier, the last thing the Rams wanted in the giant Santiago Bernabéu stadium was to concede an early goal; and, again, that is exactly what they did. After only four minutes Rod Thomas lost the ball to Martinez who scored easily. Ten minutes into the second half the Rams were shattered by two more Real goals. Martinez struck again and then Netzer sent over a free-kick for Santillana to head past Boulton. Real's goal at Derby would count double in the event of a draw and so the Rams were now trailing.

George temporarily silenced the 120,000 crowd with a good goal and the Rams were five minutes from safety when Thomas was judged to have felled Amancio, and Pirri cracked in a penalty to ensure extra-time. Nine minutes into the extra period, Santillana flicked the ball over his head, slipped between Newton and McFarland, and scored a brilliant goal. Physically and mentally drained, the Rams – with Lee suspended, Rioch out through injury, and McFarland and Newton playing only after receiving pain-killing injections – lost 5-1 and were out of the European Cup, 6-5 on aggregate.

After the Madrid game, Mackay paid Burnley £300,000 for Leighton James, their Welsh international winger. It was a Derby County record fee. In December, the Rams lost the services of Francis Lee for four games. The former England striker was also fined £200 after being found guilty of bringing the game into disrepute. On 1 November, Lee and another former England man, Leeds United's Norman Hunter, were sent off at the Baseball Ground for fighting. The battle continued as the players left the pitch and the two men had to be separated by teammates. Hunter, charged with the same offence, was cleared.

On 15 November, Derby beat West Ham 2-1 at the Baseball Ground to go top for the first time that season. But after losing 2-1 at Birmingham on 6 December, the Rams lost top spot and did not regain it. After a home defeat by Spurs on 10 January, Colin Boulton made way for former Blackburn 'keeper Graham Moseley and his run which went back to 1971 – less those three games missed through suspension and injury – came to an end. The championship race now became tense – on 25 February, the Rams drew at Old Trafford and only one point separated the top four – and Derby were also making progress in the FA Cup. The Rams reached their first semi-final since 1948. Their opponents were the same as that last hurdle of 28 years earlier, Manchester United, whose manager, Tommy Docherty, called it "the real Cup Final", adding: "What can you call the other semi-final between Crystal Palace and Southampton? It's a joke."

Saturday, 3 April 1976 goes down as a landmark in the story of Derby County. Gordon Hill scored both goals at Hillsborough as United won 2-0 (and went on to lose the Final 1-0 to "joke" team, Southampton).

The Rams could feel aggrieved, though, after what would have been an equaliser from David Nish was disallowed for offside. Nish said: "As their defence rushed out, I put the ball over the top and then collected it before it had even bounced. So you assume that no one else can be interfering with play if you play it yourself. But the referee gave someone offside on the other side of the pitch. I couldn't believe it. I don't know if the ball was in the net before he blew, but I think we were really unlucky."

Colin Boulton also had something to say about that day, even though he didn't see the game: "I never liked Dave Mackay and he never liked me. On the morning of the semi-final I should have been in the Reserves at Stoke, but the match was called off, so I went home to Cheltenham because I hadn't seen my parents for ages. Why didn't I go to Sheffield? Well, the reserve-teamers were expected to make their own way there and then pay to get in. Some of the lads actually had to stand on the terrace. On the Monday morning, Mackay hauled me in and asked me what he could have done if Graham Moseley had been injured before the start. I told him that it was up to him to ensure that I was there and, anyway, he'd made no provision for the reserve-team game had it been played and I'd been injured."

After the semi-final, the Rams faltered and their last hope of retaining the title vanished when Leicester held them to a draw at the Baseball Ground on 17 April. The season ended with a freak 6-2 win at Ipswich, where Francis Lee closed his first-class career, after exactly 500 matches, with two goals. Lee had done a magnificent job for Derby County. The Rams had finished fourth but now faced a slide that would gather speed with frightening intensity.

"Good Luck – Whoever You Are"

I N NOVEMBER 1976, Dave Mackay had been Derby County's manager for three years and one month when he asked the Rams directors for a vote of confidence. Rumours had been circulating in the town that the players were not training properly and that there was a lack of discipline.

There was certainly a problem. Despite all the previous successes under Mackay – Football League championship and a European Cup place, FA Charity Shield, FA Cup semi-finalists and a place in the UEFA Cup – Derby were now 19th in the First Division. None of what had gone before now mattered, it seemed.

When the Rams won their first match it had been in style, beating Spurs 8-2 on 16 October with four goals from makeshift centre-forward Bruce Rioch. But their European season had soon ended. After a farcical 16-1 aggregate scoreline over Irish side, Finn Harps – Hector scored five in the club record 12-0 win at the Baseball Ground – the Rams went out to AEK Athens, 5-2 on aggregate. Derby lost both legs, and goalkeeper Graham Moseley had an unhappy evening as the Rams surrendered their unbeaten home record in European competition.

In October, too, Colin Todd had added to the general unrest by seeking a transfer and, although he was later placated with a long-term contract, Derby's tale of woe was far from over. Roy McFarland was playing well enough to earn an England recall, but was then injured; and David Nish was out for the rest of the season with a knee injury. All the time the Rams dived deeper into trouble and in November, Mackay was criticised by shareholders. At the end of that month he asked for a show of hands supporting him. Instead, there was a general shuffling of feet and looking at the floor, and he was on his way, together with his assistant, Des Anderson.

Reserve-team coach Colin Murphy was given the job and there were many in the game who were surprised that Murphy, inexperienced in both playing and managerial terms, should be offered what was still one of soccer's top jobs. Within days in December, while still officially caretaker boss, Murphy was involved in two transfer deals. He sold Rioch to Everton for £180,000 and then brought Charlton's free-scoring striker, Derek Hales, for an estimated £330,000. The Hales signing was to hang like a millstone around the club's – and Murphy's – neck. In February, with Murphy now appointed officially, the Rams, led by director George Hardy, approached Brian Clough. It was a spectacular bid to bring Clough and Taylor back to the Baseball Ground, but it failed. Clough arrived to say: "Thanks, but no thanks," adding that it was the "saddest day of his life". After Derby, the pair had gone to manage Brighton before Clough, against Taylor's advice, spent a disastrous 44 days as manager of Leeds. They had been reunited at Nottingham Forest and were staying at the City Ground to honour their contracts.

In September 1976, Colin Boulton had returned from his loan spell at Southampton and was now playing well after replacing the unhappy Moseley. In March, Murphy again went into the transfer market. He sold Jeff Bourne, signed from local football for next to nothing, to Crystal Palace for £30,000, and bought Irish international midfielder Gerry Daly from Manchester United for £175,000. After fifth successive defeats, the Rams were bottom of the First Division with only 18 points. It was a bad spell into which a stylish young full-back from Dublin, David Langan, found himself pitched. But there were still First Division players at the Baseball Ground and the Rams lost only two more games. They took 19 points from the remaining 17 matches. Eleven of those games were drawn but it was enough to lift Derby clear of relegation and into 15th place. For most of the players, though, it had been a new and unpleasant experience.

Murphy was never secure in the Derby job and on 17 September 1977, he heard on television that he was to be replaced by Tommy Docherty, who had recently been sacked from Old Trafford following a well-publicised affair with the wife of United's physiotherapist. He later married her. The Doc was due to manage a Norwegian club, but the Derby job clearly held a greater attraction. "Two points from five matches" was the reason that Murphy was on his way, according to new chairman George Hardy.

Murphy and his assistant, Dario Gradi, could theoretically have stayed at the Baseball Ground. Not unnaturally, they chose to leave.

So Docherty came in, and players moved out. Archie Gemmill was one who did not want to play under the former Scotland team manager and he was quickly snapped up by Nottingham Forest in exchange for £25,000 and goalkeeper John Middleton, whose signing saw the end of Colin Boulton, the man who had made more appearances in Derby's goal than any other player. Kevin Hector was also treated shabbily after his years of yeoman service to Derby. Named as substitute for the Rams Reserves, he, too, was glad to leave the scene of his many triumphs. One player who was apparently happy to see Docherty was Charlie George. Transfer-listed at the beginning of the season, George now signed a three-year contract for The Doc, who had brought former Chelsea and England winger, Frank Blunstone, from Manchester United to work as his assistant.

Docherty was quickly into a spate of buying and selling, a frenzy of transfer activity that would ultimately leave Derby County with a shadow of its great team of the 1970s. Out went Hales, although no one was sorry about that, especially the player, who claimed that "Derby have ruined me". The Rams received £110,000 from West Ham for Hales, representing a loss for Derby of £220,00 in only nine months. Leighton James moved to QPR with Don Masson travelling in the opposite direction, and midfielders, Irish international Tony Macken and Scotsman Jeff King, both Mackay signings, rejoined their old boss who was now manager of Walsall. Thomas went to Cardiff and Moseley to Brighton after a loan period with Walsall. By Christmas, Billy Hughes, signed by Murphy from Sunderland at the start of the season, was transferred to Leicester. And in March, Notts County equalled their club record fee when they paid £45,000 for utility player David Hunt, who had played only five league games for the Rams. Into the Baseball Ground came Bohemians winger Gerry Ryan, who signed with Francis O'Brien from the Irish club for a combined fee of £60,000. Docherty had been so keen to sign Ryan that he slept the night in the sauna at a Tyneside hotel where Bohemians were staying before a UEFA Cup match against Newcastle United. O'Brien failed his medical and his part of the deal was never completed,

It was bewildering. Bruce Rioch rejoined the Rams from Everton for £150,000 – "Come and see my three Van Goghs," said Docherty of his new midfield trio of Rioch, Masson and Daly – and Forest forward Terry

Curran was the next Docherty recruit. In January, Derby paid £160,000 to Luton for left-back Steve Buckley, who they might have signed for nothing at one time because he was a product of Derbyshire non-league soccer. In February, Leicester defender, Jeff Blockley, came on loan; and in April, Docherty was reunited with Manchester United winger Gordon Hill, who came to the Baseball Ground for £250,000, claiming that he was the victim of a "vendetta" at Old Trafford.

When Liverpool arrived at the Baseball Ground in March 1978, Derby County supporters were desperately seeking a Rams' performance to lighten their gloom. Without a league win since early January, Docherty's side sat 14th in the First Division. It already seemed a lifetime since the glorious title-winning days under Clough and Mackay. Liverpool, fifth in the table, were on their way to winning another European Cup. They were also one week away from a League Cup Final against Nottingham Forest. Yet, against a team also challenging for another title, everything came right for Derby on this Wednesday evening as Daly (two goals), George and debutant Andy Crawford, a former Baseball Ground apprentice, helped the Rams to a shock 4-2 win against a team that boasted the second-best defensive record in the top flight. After the game however, Rioch had a spectacular public row with Docherty and was fined two weeks' wages and transfer-listed. Bad feeling between manager and player had been simmering for some time. Rioch had earlier been fined for allegedly leaving the pitch at Newcastle without permission. "Although he was genuinely injured, he should have given the sub time to warm up," said The Doc. After this latest row, Rioch was eventually forgiven and his suspension halved, although it was hardly kiss and make up. At the end of the season, Docherty listed Rioch and Masson, commenting of the two Scottish World Cup players: "They have proved to be poor investments". The Rams won only four more games that season and finished 12th. It was the beginning of an even darker era in the club's history.

In 1978-79, the Rams once more managed to make more headlines off the field than they did on it and most of the controversy surrounded the manager, who was suspended for seven days by the club in November following his sensational admission that he had lied under oath during a libel hearing which he had brought against Willie Morgan and Granada TV. The Rams board discussed the implications and then reinstated Docherty. But it was clear that the Derby directors were becoming increasingly concerned. Docherty also continued to make headlines in the transfer market. When he sold Colin Todd to Everton for £330,000 in September, it was his 30th transfer deal since taking over at Derby a year earlier. In that time he had sold 16 players for an estimated £1 million and bought 14 for around £1.25 million. And Docherty did not stop there. Gerry Ryan was soon on his way to Brighton for £80,000. Earlier in the season he had sold Terry Curran to Southampton, for £60,000, and Don Masson had returned to Notts County for free. In came Newcastle defender Aiden McCaffery for £45,000, Notts County forward Steve Carter, and then Docherty paid Spurs £150,000 for their Scottish striker, John Duncan. Defender Vic Moreland and forward Billy Caskey came from Glentoran, and Jonathan Clark, a young Welsh midfielder with a reputation for immense potential, from Manchester United. The Docherty transfer saga went on and on … in December, Leicester's gutsy defender David Webb, the former Chelsea star, came to the Baseball Ground for £12,000, and then Cliftonville midfield player Barney Bowers became another Docherty signing. In the New Year it was Roy Greenwood from Sunderland, and then Steve Wicks from Chelsea. Wicks cost the Rams £275,000. Meanwhile, Charlie George went to Southampton – the Rams board had blocked a move to Forest – and Rioch went on loan to Birmingham and then Sheffield United.

Still controversy raged at the Baseball Ground. Gerry Daly was transfer-listed and then suspended for two weeks, only for the Football League to tell Derby that the suspension was illegal. Then Docherty's assistant, Frank Blunstone, was fined £500 for allegedly making an illegal approach to Dundee United's international defender David Narey in an airport lounge. After gaining a mid-table position in November, December and January, the Rams slipped badly and a dreadful run in the second half of the season saw them finish 19th, only six points clear of relegation. In their last 19 league matches the Rams won only twice. In fact, they took only 10 points from a possible 38 and had a run of five successive defeats. Injuries to McFarland and Duncan, in particular, did not help, but the chopping and changing done by Docherty helped even less. Even Docherty had to confess: "When I go into the dressing-room these days, I have to ask who is playing today, and as they go out say: 'Good luck – whoever you are.'" The Doc might have thought that was funny; Derby County supporters wept at the dismantling of their great club. The transfer policy of the manager was nothing but ruinous. There were some old faces leaving the Baseball Ground at the end of the season.

David Nish's knee injury forced him to quit, while Peter Daniel, hero of the side that won the First Division title for the second time, also left in April. So did former Manchester United defender Ray Storey, who never played a league game for Derby.

Even when the Rams' season had ended, there were still shocks in store. On the eve of the FA Cup Final, Docherty announced that he was going back to Queen's Park Rangers, the club he had served for 28 days some 11 years earlier. No one was sorry to see him go. And later that month, police arrived at the Baseball Ground to conduct what would be a long investigation – for reasons that have never been made public it proved ultimately fruitless – into allegations of corrupt practice at Derby County, some of it involving player traffic between the Rams and the North American Soccer League. Could it get any worse? The answer was "Yes".

A Hair-Shirt Football Club

On 9 October 1982 barely 8,000 spectators were scattered around the Baseball Ground. Ten years earlier, more than 38,000 had hemmed in to see Benfica vanquished in the European Cup. But now the Rams were in the lower half of the Second Division, Cambridge United were proving difficult opposition, and some home players didn't seem to care. Even in the dark days of the mid-1950s, things hadn't looked this bad for Derby County, whose fortunes had worsened rapidly after Tommy Docherty's already ruinous 21 months at the club. New manager Colin Addison had a decent reputation for managing in the lower leagues, but the size of his task in trying to keep the Rams in the top flight was enormous. Addison had hardly found his desk at the Baseball Ground when the chairman who appointed him, George Hardy, was replaced by Richard Moore. The police were still nosing around as their investigation into alleged corruption continued. And club secretary, Stuart Webb, had resigned. It was hardly the best start for a new manager.

Sure enough, despite some frenzied transfer market activity in and out of the Baseball Ground – the main incomers were striker Alan Biley from Cambridge United for £350,000, and Crystal Palace centre-forward Dave Swindlehurst for a club record £410,00 after a loan deal became permanent – relegation was confirmed on the penultimate day of the season, even though the Rams beat Manchester City that day with Swindlehurst scoring. The disastrous selling of quality players by

Docherty, and his replacement of them with men of infinitely less ability, had finally taken its toll. The Rams returned to the Second Division they had left in 1969. In 1980-81, after another poor start, the Rams revived enough to finish sixth in the Second Division. Biley, who missed the last 11 games of the season through injury, would soon be off to Everton for £350,000. Duncan, potentially one of the best strikers in the game, was also dogged by injury and made only three appearances. The Rams also said goodbye to one legend, and hello again to another. Roy McFarland, also troubled by injury for much of his later career, bid farewell and went off to become player-manager of Bradford City; Kevin Hector, who had been with Vancouver Whitecaps and Burton Albion, returned, not as the striker everyone remembered, but to play in midfield. Times had certainly changed.

By Christmas 1981, the Rams had 22 points from 16 matches – this was the first season of three points for a win – before they were interrupted by bad weather and didn't play a league match from 4 December to 16 January. From the second week of the season the Rams had never been out of the bottom half of the table and after their league programme resumed with a 3-2 defeat at Orient to leave them in 17th place, Colin Addison was on his way. There was the inevitable chatter about Brian Clough returning but Addison's replacement was his assistant, the former Birmingham City centre-half, John Newman. Into the Baseball Ground came defenders John McAlle (from Everton) and Brian Attley (from Sheffield United). Best of all for the fans, though, was the return of Charlie George, although, like Hector, he would now play in the Rams' midfield. George's first home game back, against Luton Town on 27 March, attracted a crowd of 15,836, Derby County's second-highest attendance of the season. It was a boost. The last 24 matches netted the Rams 26 points and they lost only three of their last 11 matches. When Graham Taylor's high-flying Watford arrived on the final day, the Rams were not mathematically certain of avoiding relegation but a 3-1 win over the Second Division runners-up saw them finish 16th, four points clear of the drop. Hector's goal against Watford was his 201st for the Rams in his 589th – and final – appearance.

Derby County's ever-growing cash problems weren't going to be helped by another dreadful start, and on the opening day of 1982-83, the Rams lost 3-0 at home to Carlisle United in front of only 11,207 spectators. Thereafter, they slid quickly and when the first win arrived, on 8 September, there were only 8,075 at the Baseball Ground to see fellow strugglers, Chelsea, beaten 1-0. By the beginning of November, Derby were bottom of the Second Division with only eight points from their first 13 matches, and John Newman paid with his job. The Rams' debt was now said to be over £1 million and the club was so hard up that, one week, wages arrived courtesy of Rotherham United. Rotherham chairman Anton Johnson, the so-called "King of Clubs", had entered the picture and a Millmoor official turned up with the money to pay the Rams staff. But Johnson could not be involved with two clubs and eventually a new Rams chairman, Chesterfield-based snooker millionaire, Mike Watterson, had to go it alone. Watterson's appointment was followed by that of former secretary Stuart Webb to the board. Webb was not offering cash but considerable business expertise that was to stand the Rams in good stead in the years to come.

Then came Peter Taylor. Ever since he and Brian Clough resigned in October 1973, Derby County had been a difficult club to manage. The shadow of Clough, in particular, had dogged successive managers. Now, felt the fans, if one man could come to terms with the job then it was Clough's football partner who had left the City Ground for retirement six months earlier. Back in football, Taylor moved quickly. His first signing was Archie Gemmill who returned to Derby where the fans still loved him. Roy McFarland and Mick Jones were introduced as team manager and coach. McFarland needed no introduction; Jones was a steady reserve in the days of Tim Ward and the early reign of Clough. Their joint appointment at Derby caused a storm. Bradford City, their previous club, protested. The Rams were fined £10,000 and had to pay £55,000 compensation to Bradford. Taylor continued to bring in new faces – some of them old faces to football but new to the Rams. John Richards (from Wolves) and Kenny Burns (Leeds United) came on loan to join former Forest man, Gary Mills, who was on loan from NASL club, Seattle Sounders, as a Newman signing from the previous October. More permanent signings were Bobby Davison, the little striker from Halifax Town, Oldham Athletic defender Paul Futcher ("I offered him First Division vision," said Taylor) and Notts County's Paul Hooks.

But new faces meant that when the FA Cup came around, the Rams had to rely on players already on the books when the competition began. Centre-half George Foster, signed from Plymouth Argyle by Newman but ousted in favour of Futcher, and young forwards Kevin Wilson and Andy Hill, were thrown back into the fire of Cup soccer. The visit of Nottingham Forest – thanks to Clough but to the chagrin of Derby supporters now flying high in the First Division – was inevitably billed as "Clough v Taylor", although the managers played that down. After a goalless first half, Gemmill scored from a free-kick from outside the penalty area, and Andy Hill raced on to a through-ball from Mike Brolly – signed by Newman from Grimsby before the season began – to give the Rams an epic victory. A fourth-round defeat of Chelsea was marred by serious crowd trouble (a week earlier Leeds fans had wreaked similar damage on the Osmaston Stand) and although the Rams escaped lightly from an FA inquiry, it left a scar when Derby County should have been celebrating. There followed a plum fifth-round draw against Manchester United at the Baseball Ground where a crowd of 33,022 saw the Rams fight valiantly against one of Europe's best teams. In the second half young Norman Whiteside scored the only goal of the game – "Whiteside far side, onside," said a television commentator as the United man lined up to score.

It didn't really matter that the Rams were out of the FA Cup – although the cash from an Old Trafford replay would have been a godsend – because the Baseball Ground was alight again, thanks to a 15-match unbeaten run that lasted until after Burnley's visit on 30 April, when the Rams won 2-0. But in the middle of the run, Swindlehurst was transferred to West Ham – the Rams had little option since his contract was almost ended – and an NASL ruling forced Mills to return to America. Buckley was now out for the season, having broken his leg. Powell, Hooks, Gemmill and Burns were also injured, and against Blackburn and Palace, Taylor was forced to use some of the players he was trying to move on. They contributed to a brace of defeats and it was left to the Rams to beat Fulham on the last day of the season to be safe, and even then only if other results went their way.

To win promotion ahead of Leicester City, Fulham needed victory at Derby, and when Davison scored a brilliant goal in the 76th minute, it seemed that that issue at least had been settled. However, after safety gates were opened prematurely, the final 15 minutes were played out with thousands of young supporters spilling over the touchline. One of them kicked out at a Fulham player as he sped past with the ball, and when referee Ray Chadwick, a Darwen newsagent, blew for what he later said was an offside decision, everyone thought that the game had ended and supporters swarmed on to the pitch. Another Fulham player was assaulted as he fought his way to the dressing rooms, where the referee announced that there were still 78 seconds to play. Fulham appealed to have the entire game replayed but, not unnaturally, the Football League refused.

The Rams would have been safe anyway because other results had gone their way. In fact, they ended an amazing season in 13th place, far better than anyone would dared have hoped for a few weeks earlier. Steve Powell and Archie Gemmill had struggled on manfully with injuries that would have sidelined lesser mortals. Young goalkeeper Steve Cherry had performed brilliantly at times, and others who had appeared to be on their way out of the Baseball Ground shortly after Taylor arrived had fought to make him reconsider. There were some who had not responded, however, and of them Taylor could only say: "If they are at the Baseball Ground next season, then it will be an insult to our supporters." Several were released. One man who was also not at the Baseball Ground at the start of 1983-84 was Mike Watterson, who had resigned because he said he could not devote enough time to the club. John Kirkland assumed the chair.

In the summer of 1983, Taylor brought in three new players. Outside-left John Robertson, still a current Scottish international, came from Nottingham Forest for a tribunal-fixed fee of £135,000. The signing widened the rift that had existed between Clough and Taylor for some time. Sadly, the men who had together worked football miracles ended up not even speaking to each other. Bobby Campbell had done well for Roy McFarland at Bradford City and 25 Third Division goals the previous season suggested he could step up a division. His transfer cost £75,000, part of which was an interest-free loan from the management staff. The third signing was Calvin Plummer, another forward, for £10,000 from Chesterfield. Like Campbell, he did not last a season that began with a humiliating 5-0 defeat at Chelsea.

It was soon apparent that the Campbell signing was an embarrassing failure. He went back to Bradford City, the Rams losing £45,000 on the deal in a matter of weeks. Then Robertson was injured, and with the Rams suddenly also short of fit defenders, McFarland played a few games in an attempt to inspire the team. But crushing home defeats early in October confirmed it to be another season spent fighting relegation. And so it turned out, even though the signing of veteran centre-half Dave Watson, a former England regular, heralded a purple patch in November. Early December saw an amazing game against Arthur Cox's Newcastle

United, when a 2-0 half-time deficit was turned into a 3-2 victory by goals from Davison and a Gemmill penalty.

A hint of the financial problems ahead came with news that players' wages were being paid late, and final instalments on the transfers of Robertson and goalkeeper Yakka Banovic (who had signed from an Australian club in August 1980) were also overdue. By January 1984, Derby County had been banned from signing any more players, coach Mick Jones had been dismissed, and the Rams' financial problems were now enormous. The company faced bankruptcy. Debts were around £1.5 million, and on 2 February the Inland Revenue, supported by the Customs and Excise, filed a High Court winding-up petition. Derby County's bank account was frozen, and the National Westminster Bank, whose interest charges on the club's debt were soaring, now owned the Baseball Ground. Appearances in the High Court became more frequent than football matches, and yet here was a bankrupt football club, with a bottom-of-the-table team, looking to go to Wembley. An FA Cup run brought in much-needed income, although even here there was a stark reminder of the club's problems when delays in paying shares of the gate receipts to Telford United and Norwich City put the Rams in danger of being expelled from the competition.

March 1984 was the most critical month in Derby County's history. The Rams were without a win in 10 league games and a crucial High Court date was fixed for 12 March, two days after the sixth-round tie against Third Division Plymouth Argyle at Home Park. The Inland Revenue was owed PAYE sums of £131,948, and the Customs and Excise unpaid VAT of £78,123. Derby City Council and Derbyshire County Council had stayed clear of making any major cash injection, so the club needed a major backer from industry or commerce. Three new directors brought in some money and existing directors dipped into their pockets. Stuart Webb bought 27,000 shares (around 60 per cent) at a cost of £140,000, in order to offer a substantial enough package to a potential saviour from outside the club. Rumours of a multinational company based in Hong Kong came to nothing and on 1 March, Webb entered into negotiations with the millionaire publisher, Robert Maxwell, chairman of Oxford United.

On Saturday, 10 March, in the FA Cup quarter-final the Rams scrambled a goalless draw, fortunate to escape with a replay after a Plymouth shot hit both posts. Derby struggled to make an impression.

Indeed, so desperate were they that, near the end, Peter Taylor sent centre-half Dave Watson up to lead the attack where he looked sadly out of place. On Monday, 12 March, Derby County officials attended the High Court with rescue proposals, but Mr Justice Mervyn Davies was unhappy with the Maxwell package, in particular the part-payment of Inland Revenue debts. It led to a week's adjournment and pressure on the club to improve the package.

Wednesday 14 March was the blackest night in Derby County's history. At the Baseball Ground an inswinging corner by Andy Rogers evaded Steve Cherry and put Plymouth Argyle, not the Rams, into the FA Cup semi-finals. On the same day Robert Maxwell temporarily withdrew his support. However, after two further High Court adjournments, the club's directors put together an acceptable plan and the Inland Revenue and Customs and Excise had their debts met. On 12 April, at Derby County's seventh High Court appearance, the petition to wind-up the club in its centenary year was withdrawn. Peter Taylor, meanwhile, was sacked, leaving Roy McFarland with nine games to avert relegation. A more settled line-up fought hard for him, winning three of their last six matches, but it was too much to ask. Oldham Athletic did just as well. The Rams were a Third Division club for the first time since 1957. But at least they were still alive.

"Just Wring Out My Shirt ...."

I N MAY 1984, Arthur Cox had just guided Newcastle United into the First Division. Cox had a fine team at St James's Park – Keegan, Beardsley, Waddle *et al* – and apparently every reason to look forward to the new season with Newcastle in the top flight. But when the first Saturday of 1984-85 came around, Arthur Cox was managing in the Third Division – with Derby County. There had been major problems over the negotiation of a new contract with United, and Cox wasn't a man to hang around if he felt that he wasn't properly appreciated. It is to the great credit of Stuart Webb, then in his short period as Rams chairman – that he was able to persuade Cox to drop two divisions and take over at a club that had only recently avoided bankruptcy.

Cox had managerial and coaching experience far beyond the average 44-year-old. After a broken leg ended his playing career when he was an 18-year-old with Coventry City, Cox coached Coventry's youth team, and then worked for Walsall and Aston Villa as chief coach and Halifax Town as assistant manager. In the 1970s, Preston won the Third Division title when Cox was their chief coach, and Sunderland lifted the FA Cup and the Second Division championship when he was assistant manager to Bob Stokoe. After a short stint with Galatasaray of Turkey, Cox was appointed manager of Chesterfield and took them to within a point of promotion to the Second Division. Then came Newcastle United. His long apprenticeship in management had earned him a reputation as a hardworking disciplinarian.

At the Baseball Ground, Cox asked Roy McFarland to remain as his assistant, and in his first season the Rams finished seventh in the Third Division. They had been in the promotion-chasing pack, but after a workmanlike defeat of York City on New Year's Day, it was another two months before the next league win. It was, though, a decent enough position. After the rapid tumble of the previous five years, stability was welcome.

Before the centenary season, Ian Maxwell, son of Robert, had become chairman of Derby County. Part of that deal was the purchase of the Baseball Ground from the NatWest Bank for £305,000. The bank agreed to forego the £750,000 overdraft. That was a relief. But it didn't mean that the new Derby manager suddenly had unlimited funds at his disposal. Far from it: goalkeeper Eric Steele and full-back Charlie Palmer (both from Watford) and centre-half Rob Hindmarch (Sunderland) came on free transfers. They were all successful at Derby, though. Of Hindmarch, Cox said: "I'd have signed him even if I'd still been at Newcastle and in the First Division."

Kevin Wilson, who'd joined the Rams from non-League football in 1979, scored 13 goals in 14 Third Division and Milk Cup games before he broke his left arm early in the game against Plymouth in October. When Wilson was fit again, Cox sold him to First Division Ipswich Town for £150,000, money the manager put towards the transfers of Trevor Christie from Nottingham Forest for £100,000 (Christie's goals had helped Notts County into the First Division in 1981); Gary Micklewhite, a First Division midfielder who had played in an FA Cup Final, from Queen's Park Rangers for £80,000; and, just before the transfer deadline, Geraint Williams, a Welsh Under-23 midfielder, was signed for £40,000 from Bristol Rovers. After Wilson's departure, much depended on Bobby Davison who during the next five months responded with half the team's goals – 16 of 32 – which made him the obvious choice for the supporters' Player of the Year. The 1984-85 season also marked the final appearance of the injury-plagued Steve Powell after 420 senior games for the Rams that stretched back to his debut as a 16-year-old in that glorious League championship-winning season of 1971-72.

In July 1985, Cox strengthened his squad further with goalkeeper Mark Wallington from Leicester City (£25,000), defender Ross MacLaren from Shrewsbury Town (£67,000), midfielder Steve McClaren from Hull City (£70,000) and Republic of Ireland outside-left Jeff Chandler from Bolton Wanderers (for £38,000, the fee set by a tribunal much to Bolton's annoyance). Only Steve Buckley, Bobby Davison, Paul Blades, Graham Harbey, Dick Pratley and Andy Garner now remained from the pre-Cox days as the Rams found themselves 5/1 favourites for the Third Division championship. But 10 points from the first eight games

Rams dish out a drubbing to the Swans

WHEN Swansea City visited the Baseball Ground on the first Wednesday of October 1985, Rams manager Arthur Cox was looking for a special response from his players.

Cox would not be disappointed. Four first-half goals settled Derby's nerves and set them on their way back to the old Second Division.

The result was a foregone conclusion as early as the 26th minute, by which time the Rams were 3-0 up. In fact, it took them only 71 seconds to get their noses in front.

Gary Micklewhite collected a Swansea clearance and lobbed the ball over to Bobby Davison, who chested it down and sent it into the net off Swansea's Paul Price. There was no dubious goals panel in those days, and Davison claimed the goal on the very proper grounds that his shot was going in anyway. It was his 50th goal for the Rams.

It was a great start, but the Rams needed to consolidate it, and after 20 minutes came the second goal. Jeff Chandler swung over a corner, Ross MacLaren headed it on, and Trevor Christie steered it over the line.

Six minutes later, MacLaren sent over a low centre and Davison was on hand to sweep it into the net. Three minutes from half-time, it was Davison who had a big hand in goal number four.

First he robbed Tommy Hutchison, then accepted a return pass from Micklewhite to fire a shot at Jimmy Rimmer. The goalkeeper could only parry the ball, and there was the tireless Micklewhite to make it 4-0 before the kettle had boiled for the half-time tea.

As is often the case, an avalanche of first-half goals was not followed by a hatful in the second half. Indeed, only four minutes after the restart, the Rams were caught napping when they failed to clear Colin Pascoe's centre and Gary Emmanuel made it 4-1.

But there was never going to be a dramatic Swansea fightback. In fact, their goalscorer, Emmanuel, helped to give Derby an immediate chance to restore their four-goal lead.

Trying to head the ball back to Rimmer, he succeeded only in giving Davison a great opportunity to make it 5-1, but the Swans' goalkeeper bowled him over instead. The referee pointed to the spot, but MacLaren hit the penalty too close to Rimmer, who was able to turn it round his post.

After 63 minutes, however, the Rams did get a fifth goal, when Chandler – a real handful on this night – was played through by Davison. As Rimmer came out to narrow the angle, Chandler chipped the ball so delicately over the goalkeeper's head to put the icing on the Rams' cake.

In the *Derby Evening Telegraph*, Gerald Mortimer wrote: "There were times when the crowd, wanting ten, chuntered at the Rams, but they stood to applaud them off after a display which had promotion written across it."

was not promotion form. At the end of September, though, Derby beat First Division Leicester City 2-0 in the first leg of a Milk Cup tie and that was the turning point. A 1-1 draw at the Baseball Ground in the return leg showed that the Rams' giantkilling performance at Filbert Street had been no fluke and although they went out in the next round, 2-1 at home to Forest, their league form settled into top gear.

When Steve McClaren was injured in November, Cox signed John Gregory for £100,000 from Queen's Park Rangers. Gregory was an England international who had played alongside Micklewhite in the 1982 FA Cup Final. The Rams now put together an unbeaten run that coincided with the FA Cup. Crewe were beaten 5-1, Telford United 6-1 Gillingham 3-1 in replay, and Sheffield United 1-0. The Wembley trail eventually came to an end on a bone-hard pitch at Hillsborough where Sheffield Wednesday won 2-0. The Rams' good league run continued, however, and they needed two points from their final two games for promotion.

Supporters were in for a nail-biting home finale. Against Rotherham United on 9 May 1986, substitute Phil Gee scored after 77 minutes but Rotherham equalised almost immediately. With five minutes to play, the Rams won a free-kick on the edge of the penalty area. Rotherham's Dungworth was sent off. Jeff Chandler joined the Rotherham players, only to be jostled and pushed. The last push came after the free-kick was taken. The referee awarded a penalty. Trevor Christie stepped up and shot left-footed, inside the post to the goalkeeper's right. The Rams won 2-1. Defeat at Darlington on the last day of the season didn't matter. Derby had pipped Wigan Athletic for the third promotion spot. By this time, Derby County Reserves, skippered by Dick Pratley, had won the Central League, the first time the title had gone to a Third Division club.

Things were looking up. And there was more to come, even though the Rams opened 1986-87 with a 1-0 defeat at the hands of Oldham Athletic at the Baseball Ground. As often happens, the opening day's result was a poor predictor of the final placing, and it proved to be Derby's only home league defeat of the season. Once again Cox had improved the team with new signings, especially full-backs Mel Sage from Gillingham (£60,000) and Michael Forsyth, who came from West Brom the previous March (£26,000) while Steve Cross signed from Shrewsbury Town (£60,000). Mark Lillis, from Manchester City (£200,000; Christie, who was valued at £100,000, went to City as part of the deal), had early misfortune with injuries. After Crystal Palace's Mickey Droy clobbered Lillis early in

September, former painter and decorator Phil Gee, 21, a bargain from non-League Gresley Rovers at an eventual cost of £5,000, began to show a two-footed appetite for Second Division goals.

The season began to spark at the end of September, and by the beginning of November the Rams were seventh, and fourth a month later. The day after Boxing Day, after turning a 2-0 deficit at home to Barnsley into a 3-2 victory, they topped the Second Division in what was becoming the most open promotion race for years. After a quiet January – due to bad weather the Rams played only two league games – Derby slipped slightly. Then winger Nigel Callaghan arrived from Watford for £140,000, some of the money coming from Charlie Palmer's move to Hull. Callaghan was moving to a club in a lower division, and, like Gregory, Micklewhite, Christie, Lillis, MacLaren and Wallington before him, said he was persuaded by the club's potential – and probably the "First Division wages" that Derby were rumoured to be paying.

After beating Blackburn 3-2 on 18 March, the Rams went top of the table again and this time they stayed there. Their away wins reached a club record 11. In the previous 20 years, only Birmingham (1984-85) and Blackpool (1967-68) had won more away games in the Second Division. Unbeaten for 13 league games, the Rams eventually tasted defeat again on 17 April, at Blackburn where Simon Garner's two goals took him to 11 in nine games against the Rams. But Derby County were awash in success and the Reserves had lost only one of their last 18 games. A second successive Central League championship proved only a few points out of range. Back in Division Two, a brave diving header by Lillis, his first and only goal for the club, beat Bradford City, and a 2-1 win against Leeds United made certain of promotion to the First Division with two games still remaining. The Rams needed a point to ensure the championship. They could have picked it up at Reading but lost 2-1. Never mind, the title could be won in front of the home fans, over 20,000 of them in fact. A goal down to Plymouth, the Rams produced the season's final recovery to score three times in the last 10 minutes and win 4-2. Arthur Cox, Bell's Second Division Manager of the Year, told *Ram Magazine* editor Harry Brown: "You can find my secret by wringing out my shirt at the end of every working day." Indeed, everyone had worked hard, not least Gregory, MacLaren and Micklewhite who were all ever-present, the latter two having played in all 88 league games of two successive promotion seasons that had carried Derby County from the Third to the First.

Captain Bob

The seven-year exile from the First Division was over. From the dark depths of Third Division football and the brink of bankruptcy, Derby County were back among the game's elite. There wasn't the euphoria that had surrounded the Clough-Taylor achievement of 1969, nor the "this-is-where-we-belong" confidence of the early post-war years. This time it was more a sense of relief that supporters felt. But they were still going to be treated to some memorable moments, not least when on 25 June 1987, Robert Maxwell, the new Rams chairman, announced that Derby County had signed England's 37-year-old goalkeeper, Peter Shilton. It was claimed to be a £1 million transfer, but that was typical Maxwell spin. Less than £100,000 went to Southampton. The rest needed Derby to win everything over the next three years. Then another England star, centre-half Mark Wright, arrived from Southampton, for £760,000. This time that was the actual fee. Derby County had never paid so much for a player. The message was clear – only the best would do. But Maxwell had conditions: immaculate crowd behaviour, and an average home attendance of more than 20,000.

On 26 September, Maxwell flew in to see his first game at the Baseball Ground. Derby lost 1-0 to Oxford United, and Maxwell left well before the end. Rams supporters became used to seeing his helicopter taking off again from behind the main stand just after half-time. That is on the days that the owner bothered to turn up, which wasn't very often. He was still issuing edicts, though. Not least reminding everyone that in order to maintain a squad of high-quality players, he needed to see regular 20,000-plus home attendances. The Oxford game was the fifth at home that season. The Rams had won only two, and the average attendance was 15,804.

So instead of more new signings, players were moved out. Lillis went to Aston Villa for £130,000, Davison to Leeds United for £350,000. Then Maxwell tried to buy Watford from Elton John. The Football League put a stop to that, but while that was sorted out, Derby County could not deal in the transfer market. In mid-November, the home game against Chelsea was shown live on television. Maxwell turned up and plonked himself in the centre of a team photograph. Early in December, Watford drew 1-1 at the Baseball Ground, Mark Wright's goal helping to extend the Rams' unbeaten run to five games. The average attendance was now 16,701.

With Davison transferred, Gee finding goals much harder to come by in the First Division, and Micklewhite out for six months with an Achilles' tendon injury, the attack relied heavily on Nigel Callaghan. Then there came a dreadful spell. Between 12 December and 10 February the Rams suffered eight successive league defeats – the last seven by the odd goal – plus Chelsea knocked them out of the FA Cup. It was an unwanted club record. At the end of January, the signing of former Glasgow Rangers forward, Ted "The Tin Man" McMinn, from Seville for £300,000, provided a fillip. On his home debut, against Manchester United – a game that at last brought the first 20,000 attendance of the season – McMinn scored with a stunning 30-yarder. Unfortunately he was soon to undergo a hernia operation and within two months the Rams had slumped to fourth from bottom – a play-off position when relegation-threatened clubs were included in the end-of-season bunfight – and the average home attendance was 16,948, even after the boost from the Manchester United game.

On 27 February, a 1-0 victory over West Ham was the Rams' first win for three months. The 2-1 win against Newcastle United on 4 April was only the second at home in over four months. Then came news that Maxwell had invited former Holland star Johan Cruyff to be Derby County's new technical director. Arthur Cox, having learned this from Maxwell's *Daily Mirror* – was it simply a publicity stunt? – uncharacteristically hit out at his chairman. When Stuart Webb approached Ian Maxwell about the situation, after Robert Maxwell had ordered Webb to arrange a press conference in Derby for the Monday so that he (Maxwell senior) could announce the Cruyff appointment, the Rams director was told not to worry, Robert Maxwell would be in the USA on Monday. It was just the owner playing games.

Former Arsenal striker Frank Stapleton came on loan from Ajax Amsterdam but a home defeat by QPR restored relegation worries with three matches left. Victory over Southampton (where Shilton set a record with his 825th Football League appearance) and two excellent draws – at Watford and at home to Everton – saw the Rams finish 15th and out of the play-offs by a point. It was obvious where the weakness was: Gregory and Gee each had the lowest tally (six league goals) of any Rams top goalscorer in history.

The £1 million signing of striker Dean Saunders from Oxford United in October 1988 went a long way to solving the problem. The Rams finished fifth in the First Division in 1988-89, their best league placing since Dave Mackay's last full season of 1975-76, and Saunders was leading scorer with 14. Cox's five years in charge had showed continued improvement, and despite not providing those elusive 20,000-plus attendances, supporters were becoming accustomed to close-season signings. In 1988 it was Trevor Hebberd from Oxford for £275,000 (including Mickey Lewis in part-exchange) to take over from the departing John Gregory who went to coach Portsmouth, Paul Goddard from Newcastle for £425,000, and Nick Pickering from Coventry for £250,000. When Andy Garner left for Blackpool in August 1988, Paul Blades was the sole survivor of the pre-Cox days.

When Arsenal visited the Baseball Ground on 26 November, the Rams were sixth, the Gunners second. Michael Thomas gave Arsenal the lead but Callaghan (who in February would leave for Aston Villa for £500,00) followed up McMinn's penalty equaliser and Gee volleyed a spectacular 78th-minute winner. Derby went fifth, and the title race was still open, but in December there were three home defeats. The Rams won more points away from the Baseball Ground, going more than five months – from early September to mid-February – without a league defeat on opponents' grounds. The best away performance came in the penultimate match, at Arsenal who were challenging for the title. Saunders scored twice (one a penalty) before a late goal by Alan Smith made it a neat 2-1 double. The Rams had set up the most dramatic finish in the history of the Football League, Arsenal scoring with the last kick of the season at Anfield to win the title from Liverpool by the narrowest possible margin (more goals with goal-difference equal). On 15 April the Hillsborough Disaster, that ultimately claimed 96 lives, had seen Derby County moved quickly. Fans would never again watch football at the Baseball Ground from behind a fence.

All in all, it had been an eventful season, albeit one with the usual Robert Maxwell controversy. In January 1989, Maxwell had introduced two Czech internationals, Lubos Kubic and Ivo Knoflicek, to a London press conference. The players had defected while on tour with Slavia Prague in the summer of 1988 – the Iron Curtain was still drawn across Europe – and now they moved to Derby and were introduced to the crowd before an FA Cup match against Southampton. But FIFA refused to sanction the move without a transfer fee. Maxwell, a Czech by birth, might have felt a loss of face. The Czechs never played for Derby and there were allegations in a Sunday newspaper that there had been some underhand business involved in their signings, including forged documents. It was typical of the web of intrigue that Robert Maxwell weaved.

Derby County's debt was now around £2 million, so there would be no more costly signings, although before the start of 1989-90 Arthur Cox was happy to sign a new five-year contract. With people's minds still on the Hillsborough Disaster, the game against Manchester United on 26 August was delayed by 25 minutes when United fans in the 22,175 crowd pushed and pulled on the terrace behind the Osmaston End goal. Indeed, United fans seemed to be popping up all over the Baseball Ground. They were urged back by Derbyshire-born Michael Knighton, the man hoping to take over the Old Trafford club. The deal fell through because, so far as United were concerned, there was less to Knighton than met the eye. But when he was later owner of Carlisle United, it was Knighton who paid enough for Steve Bloomer's international caps to allow a memorial to the great Rams player to be erected in Derby's Lock Up Yard.

Against United, goals by Saunders (penalty) and Goddard suggested that the Rams, unbeaten in their first three games, would again be a force. By November, however, they were fourth from bottom when they faced Manchester City at the Baseball Ground. City's offside trap came unstuck that day and the Rams scored six. Then bottom-of-the-table Sheffield Wednesday were beaten 2-0, and McMinn got two against West Brom, taking the Rams into the last eight of the Littlewoods Cup. Ten Baseball Ground goals in 12 days and none conceded – this was good stuff. But McMinn damaged knee ligaments and needed an operation. In December, Micklewhite also damaged knee ligaments and was sidelined for a lengthy spell. Then Paul Goddard was suddenly transferred to Millwall for £800,000, a remarkable fee for such a move. Mick Harford – £480,000 from Luton Town – was signed to replace Goddard but his first game was lost to Nottingham Forest before a run of seven games without a win was ended with the 2-0 victory – two Harford headers – that sent Millwall into the Second Division. The Rams finished 16th and, lacking money for new men, Arthur Cox looked back on a season when seven young Rams players appeared in league football for the first time. There was still experience, though. In the summer, England reached the World Cup semi-finals with Shilton, taking his number of England caps to 125, and Wright both playing major roles.

A week into the 1990-91 season Robert Maxwell announced that Derby County was for sale. The price was £8 million. Was the club worth it? When Wimbledon came to the Baseball Ground for the third league game of the season, the attendance was only 12,469. When the Rams lost at Anfield on 6 October, it was their fifth defeat in a row. No wonder they were bottom of the table. The season was two months old before Derby won a league match, 1-0 at Southampton. No new players were signed, despite the departure of Blades to Norwich City for £700,000 and Hindmarch to Wolves for £300,000. Victory over Luton and a goalless draw with Manchester United showed recovery, and then wins over Forest and at Sunderland took the Rams out of the relegation zone. The relief was short lived. The visit of Chelsea on 15 December produced 10 goals. It was exciting – but it was also the first time for over 31 years that the Rams had conceded six at home.

There had been little response to the "for sale" sign at Derby County. An offer by local newspaper millionaire Lionel Pickering was rejected. Pickering had tired of waiting for an answer and went public. He was then told that he was no longer welcome at the Baseball Ground. Rams supporters turned on Maxwell who claimed that the local media incited the fans, and BBC Radio Derby commentator Graham Richards was barred from the Baseball Ground. Maxwell wrote an open latter to one of his critics, the editor of the *Derby Evening Telegraph:* "The reason we have not maintained our progress over the last two years is that we have not had matching support from enough fans and we continue to have the local media conducting its long-standing vendetta against the club and those who run it."

The return of Ted McMinn after a 14-month lay-off was welcomed, but the Rams were going to win only one of their last 23 matches, and when Liverpool arrived at the Baseball Ground on 23 March it marked a new low as Derby lost 7-1. On 16 April, with relegation already only one game away, Robert Maxwell confirmed that Saunders and Wright would leave at the end of the season. On 4 May, Derby at last managed a win, 6-2 against Southampton with a hat trick for former youth team player Paul Williams. It still left the Rams rock bottom. They finished 10 points adrift of Sunderland, the other relegated side. Saunders was Player of the Year, his 17 league goals in a desperately struggling team an outstanding performance.

Relegation meant a fall in the price of the club – down to £5 million. Both Peter Gadsby, chairman and managing director of the Derby-based construction company, Birch plc, and the current board put in offers. Eventually, Gadsby joined forces with the board. The new chairman would be Brian Fearn, while Gadsby and Stuart Webb would be joint deputy chairmen. Meanwhile, Mark Wright (£2.2 million) and Dean Saunders (£2.9 million) were transferred to Liverpool. The Saunders fee was a record between two British clubs although 10 per cent of Derby's profit of £1.9 million went to Oxford United, his previous club. In any case, Derby County wouldn't see any of the money. That was destined for Robert Maxwell, who didn't come to wave goodbye. His helicopter had broken down. Six months later Maxwell mysteriously disappeared from his yacht, the *Lady Ghislaine,* and was found in the sea near the Canary Islands. His death left massive financial problems for just about everyone who had ever been involved with him, and there was relief that the Rams had disentangled themselves just in time. At least we now knew why he suddenly lost interest in all things Derby County.

Play-off fever

On Thursday, 21 November 1991, Lionel Pickering became majority shareholder of Derby County. It was agreed that Pickering, former owner of the Trader Group of newspapers, and a Rams fan from the Carter-Doherty days, would ultimately have more than three-quarters of the shares and complete control. The club's debts were cleared, £300,000 a year in interest saved, and money was made available to Arthur Cox who, before the start of the season, had joined the board of directors. The Rams had already signed Aston Villa's 23-year-old centre-half Andy Comyn, for £200,000, and Middlesbrough's central defender Simon Coleman, also 23, for £300,000. The money had to come from somewhere and it wasn't long before Harford had returned to Luton for £350,000, and Cross had been sold to Bristol Rovers for £75,000. But then Lionel Pickering arrived and there was no need to wheel and deal in order to sign new players. The new owner simply dipped into his own pocket.

Yet towards the end of 1991 there seemed little need for big signings. After only two wins in the first eight league games, by 16 November the Rams, now captained by Geraint Williams, went third in the Second Division. The revival coincided with the arrival of two strikers: former Rams favourite, Bobby Davison, returned on loan from Leeds; and 6ft 5in Ian Ormondroyd came on loan from Aston Villa before being signed for £300,000 at the end of December. Ormondroyd's stay was a short one, though, and a towering header at Filbert Street caught Leicester City's attention. Before a knee injury ended his loan spell, Davison scored eight goals in 10 league games, which took his Derby County tally to 106, making him one of only 10 players to score a century of goals for the club.

By the end of January the Rams had gathered 22 points from 13 away games but only 17 points from 13 home games. Then the manager began to spend the owner's money: 24-year-old Marco Gabbiadini, from Crystal Palace for £1 million, and 25-year-old Paul Simpson from Oxford United for £500,000. Each scored on his debut, Gabbiadini in the 1-0 win at Portsmouth, Simpson in the 2-1 win at Leicester.

When Shilton left to become player-manager of Plymouth Argyle in March, Steve Sutton, who had previously been at Derby on loan, came from Nottingham Forest for £300,000. Then supporters began to see the real measure of what Lionel Pickering was prepared to do for Derby County. The signing of 21-year-old forward Paul Kitson, from Leicester City set a new record fee for the Rams. Kitson was valued at £1.3 million with Gee and Ormondroyd going the other way as £500,000 worth of the deal. Striker Tommy Johnson, 21, came from Notts County, initially on loan, later permanently for £1,375,000. Defender Shane Nicholson, also 21, arrived from Lincoln City for £80,000.

It was money well spent. The Rams' total of away wins was taken to a record 12, and automatic promotion to the newly forming FA Premier League depended on the final day of the regular season. The Rams did their bit, winning 2-1 at Swindon, but 10-man Middlesbrough overhauled a 1-0 deficit to win at Wolves. Derby had to settle for third place and a first appearance in a modern-day play-off. In the first leg of the semi-final, defensive errors at Ewood Park turned an early 2-0 lead into a 4-2 defeat. At the Baseball Ground, Andy Comyn, the Rams' only ever-present with 56 League and Cup starts, dived to head the first goal after 23 minutes, but Kevin Moran's equaliser for Blackburn, early in the second half, gave Derby an uphill fight. The Rams had to wait until the 76th minute before McMinn's goal raised the tempo for the finale. Derby needed another to take the game to extra-time. Forsyth hit the bar, and Paul Williams went close, but the 2-1 win was not enough to earn a play-off Final at Wembley. Blackburn went through, 5-4 on aggregate. Three years later they would win the Premier League.

Again Lionel Pickering dipped into his pocket. During the summer Welsh international midfielder Mark Pembridge (£1.25 million from Luton) and centre-half Darren Wassall (£600,000 from Nottingham Forest) arrived. In September came midfielder Martin Kuhl (£650,000

Gee Whizz in a Villa Thriller

DERBY County's FA Cup-tie against Aston Villa on 5 February 1992 had practically everything – seven goals including a stunning effort by Paul Williams, penalty dramas, even a sending off. The only blot on such a remarkable evening was that it was Villa, not Derby, who went through to the fifth round.

Evening games at the Baseball Ground always seemed to have that extra crackle, and the visit of Ron Atkinson's side was no exception. Villa stood sixth in the top flight, the Rams 11th in the second tier after being relegated the previous season.

With only five minutes played, the old ground erupted when the Rams, attacking the Osmaston end, took the lead. Martyn Chalk, who had already fired over the bar, got the ball out to Ted McMinn. Villa's goalkeeper, Les Sealey, could not hold McMinn's shot, and Phil Gee, so desperate for a good performance, knocked it over the line.

Derby could not have hoped for a better start, but 18 minutes later they trailed 3-1, their dreams of a shock result now apparently dashed.

In the ninth minute, Kevin Richardson took a corner and Dwight Yorke equalised from Paul McGrath's flick on. Ten minutes later, it was Yorke who put Villa in front, although Peter Shilton appeared to have been impeded as he came out for Steve Froggat's corner.

In the 23rd minute, the Rams looked to be on their way out of the Cup when Garry Parker hammered a spectacular shot past Shilton, who seemed rooted to the spot.

Seven minutes before half-time, however, McMinn and Geraint Williams combined, and Gee finished off the move with a powerful header into Sealey's net.

This was turning into a remarkable Cup-tie – and the drama was far from over. Before half-time, Simon Coleman brought down Yorke after Shilton had failed to deal with an awkward ball, but the Rams goalkeeper partially redeemed himself by blocking Yorke's penalty. Alas, the Villa winger hit home the rebound and Derby were again two goals adrift.

Twelve minutes into the second half, Villa were awarded another penalty when Coleman handled Richardson's free-kick. This time Shilton not only stopped Yorke's spot kick, he held on to the ball.

It was a vital save because within two minutes, the Rams had pulled back to 4-3 with a brilliant goal. After a Jason Kavanagh free-kick, Chalk crossed the ball and there was Paul Williams to hook a spectacular volley into the net.

With 15 minutes to play, Villa's Polish international, Dariusz Kubucki, who had already been booked along with McGrath, body-checked McMinn and was ordered off.

The closing minutes were real nail-biters. Paul Williams and Gee both went close for the Rams, while Daley hit the woodwork for ten-men Villa. It had been a magnificent Cup-tie. At the final whistle, both teams received a standing ovation from a crowd of 22,452.

from Portsmouth), Dutch midfielder Richard Goulooze (£100,000 from Heerenveen) and centre-half Craig Short (£2.5 million from Notts County). The Short signing was the third time inside six months that Cox had broken the club record, this time almost doubling the fees spent on Kitson and Johnson. It brought Lionel Pickering's total outlay on behalf of Derby County to £9.6 million in eight months.

Yet it was still not enough to get Derby County back into the top flight. After a dreadful start to 1992-93 – they didn't win a game until the end of September – the Rams finished eighth. A run of away victories was taken to a club-record seven. But there was also a club record of 10 home league defeats in a season (as early as 20 February). It was bizarre that the same team could break club records for most successive away wins and most home defeats in the same season. Kitson scored 23 goals in all games, the best Rams' return since Bobby Davison's 26 in 1984-85, although 24 of Davison's were in the league, whereas Kitson managed only 17 there. The most notable absentee was Geraint Williams who, after missing the 1991-92 run-in through injury, had joined Premier League newcomers Ipswich Town for £650,000. Williams had made 332 senor appearances for Derby who he had served magnificently. The Rams did reach the FA Cup quarter-finals in 1992-93, losing a Hillsborough replay. They also appeared in the Anglo-Italian Cup Final, losing 3-1 to Cremonese in front of a Wembley crowd of 37,024, most of them from Derby and most of them wishing that they could exchange that season's cup days out for promotion. One trophy did come to the Baseball Ground – the Reserves won the Pontins League Division Two.

By the summer of 1993, Arthur Cox had been Derby County manager for nine years, which made him the longest-serving Rams boss since George Jobey. His achievements were admirable. However, his expensive team would be scrutinised every minute of the new season. The start was good – a 5-0 home win against Sunderland – and in the first week the Rams fielded two more big signings – England right-back Gary Charles (£725,000 from Nottingham Forest) and USA defender or midfielder John Harkes (from Sheffield Wednesday for a fee thought to be £800,000). Some of the money came from summer sales – Comyn to Plymouth (£200,000), McMinn to Birmingham (£115,000), Mark Patterson to Plymouth (£100,000) – but most hadn't. Lionel Pickering had been generous again. Promotion, though, needed to come quickly because for the 12 months to 31 May 1993 the club showed a trading deficit of over £1 million. According to chairman Brian Fearn, the shortfall was due to the club "assembling a Premiership squad on First Division income".

Supporters were also now questioning Cox's tactics. One thing that was beginning to annoy fans was the manager's insistence that every Rams player should be in the penalty area to defend a corner. Some pointed out that it was becoming increasingly difficult to get the ball downfield again. "We attack as a team, we defend as a team," explained the manager. There now seemed something of a siege mentally at the Baseball Ground. BBC Radio Derby had long since alienated Cox, who now refused to speak to them, while supporters worried that the millions bankrolled by Lionel Pickering had been spent on potential that had yet to be realised and, indeed, perhaps looked as if it might never be.

On the second weekend of the season, as the Rams went down 3-0 at Ayresome Park where Wassall was dismissed, it was reported that Arthur Cox was immobilised with a severe back injury. Roy McFarland deputised during September and took the Rams to halfway in the division. Then, on Saturday 2 October, came the announcement that Cox had resigned through ill health. He had been manager for a total of nine years, and much of his reign had restored the dignity of being a Rams fan. Cox would also argue that he had brought some fine players to the club and that his legacy was a young team with much promise. Whatever else, the owner would get his money back with interest when the players were finally sold on.

McFarland's first game as manager was at home to West Brom. Goalless at half-time, the match took off in the second half and went out of control with goal after goal – eight inside half an hour. Derby won 5-3. Home form was now more productive but the Rams couldn't win away, a complete turnaround from the previous season. Then two successive away victories were followed by a calamitous home defeat. On 7 November a home win would have taken the Rams to the top of a tight division, but Wolves' Steve Bull scored all four goals at the Baseball Ground.

There were two significant departures – Coleman for £250,000 to Sheffield Wednesday after a loan spell, and midfielder Craig Ramage, a Derby lad, to Watford for £90,000. McFarland and chief scout Alan Durban were looking for senior professionals who could help nurture their young team. In the New Year, 35-year-old Gordon Cowans (£75,000 from Aston Villa) and 33-year-old former Everton star Kevin Ratcliffe (who had been with Second Division Cardiff City and had not played league football since September) joined the Rams. Cowans had won 10 England caps, Ratcliffe 59 for Wales. Ratcliffe was not overly impressed with his new colleagues. "A club full of spoilt kids who got too much too soon," was his comment to *The Independent* two years later. "They thought they knew everything when they were still learning the game."

Defeat at Southend on the final day condemned the Rams to the fourth and final play-off spot. That brought Mick McCarthy's Millwall to the Baseball Ground, where Derby won more convincingly than the 2-0 scoreline suggested. The second leg at the New Den made national news – but not for the football. The Rams won 3-1 but there were two lengthy stoppages because of pitch invasions. Goalkeeper Martin Taylor was knocked over by spectators, and near the end McFarland substituted his two black players, Charles and Williams, for their own safety. There were more ugly scenes outside the ground. A BBC Radio Derby car was turned on its roof, and coaches carrying Derby supporters were stoned. After the game at Derby, Millwall's chairman, Reg Burr, had accused the Rams of "kicking us off the park". And in his programme notes, McCarthy had written: "Derby fans managed to make it a hostile environment for us up there and I know from experience that they cannot hold a candle to the Millwall crowd in this department." None of it was helpful but although an FA enquiry found Millwall FC guilty of failing to control the crowd, punishments were suspended for two years.

The only blemish in the Rams' build-up to the play-off Final against Leicester City at Wembley was Shane Nicholson's 16-hour detention at Full Street police station after an incident at 2am on the eve of the game. This breach of club discipline cost Nicholson his place in the squad. A crowd of 73,671 saw the Rams dominate the first half-hour but score only once, in the 27th minute through Tommy Johnson who was enjoying his best season for Derby with 19 goals in all competitions. Almost on the stroke of half-time Leicester equalised. Taylor came for a deep cross from the right and was clattered by Iwan Roberts, an action that even Roberts thought worthy of a free-kick to Derby instead of Steve Walsh heading Leicester level. Three minutes from time came heartbreak for Rams fans and the loss of £3 million worth of Premier League money for Derby County: Simon Grayson crossed from the Leicester right and Ian Ormondroyd sent in a fine header that produced an even finer save from Taylor. Unfortunately, Walsh knocked in the loose ball. For Rams supporters there was only the prospect of a long and empty-handed journey home.

A bad start to 1994-95 – bottom of the table after four games – was the prelude to boardroom drama that was typical Derby County. The on-off-on £2.25 million transfer of Paul Kitson to Newcastle United – Kitson had earlier been left out of the team after he criticised Derby County in a national newspaper article – saw chairman Brian Fearn and owner Lionel Pickering bitterly opposed to each other. An Emergency General Meeting on 27 October gave Pickering absolute control over the appointment and dismissal of directors. The inevitable outcome was that majority shareholder Pickering took over as chairman, and Fearn, Bill Hart and Colin McKerrow left the board. Mike Horton resigned as a director to concentrate on Derbyshire County Cricket Club. Peter Gadsby became vice-chairman of the Rams and Stuart Webb returned to the board. After 25 years at Derby County in various capacities, general manager Michael Dunford became Everton's chief executive.

Prior to the Kitson sale, there had been other departures. Ratcliffe left to become player-coach at Chester City, Martyn Chalk (who had signed from non-League football on the same day that Mick Harford joined the Rams) moved to Stockport County, and Goulooze signed for Cambour-Leeuwarden. Kuhl might have gone to Notts County but his loan period was spoiled by a caution in his first game and a sending-off in his second. Cowans succeeded Kuhl as club captain, while Alan Durban moved to assistant manager and Ron Jukes came in as chief scout. Midfielder Steve Hodge came from Leeds on loan and helped the Rams rise from bottom to sixth during September but in mid-October, at Southend, Martin Taylor suffered a double fracture of his left leg. In the same game Pembridge suffered a serious knee injury and was to miss the next four months.

The October Emergency General Meeting took place with the Rams in 18th position in Division One, and the Big Spenders were now the Big Sellers. In 12 months to the end of January 1995, Roy McFarland had sold 10 senior players for £6 million. Cowans went to Wolves, just before Christmas, for a conditional fee worth up to £30,000. The biggest news was the joint deal that took Johnson (£2 million) and Charles (£900,000) to Aston Villa, while Kuhl went to Bristol City for £350,000 and forward Dean Sturridge was exchanged for Torquay United defender Paul Trollope, both on loan. Trollope later joined the Rams for a bargain £100,000 fee. Paul Williams took over the captaincy from Cowans. The signing of Dean Yates, from Notts County in January – the fee was decided by a tribunal and could eventually add up to £800,000 if he played enough games for the Rams – provided McFarland with a powerful back three of Yates, Williams and Short, although Yates was to suffer a cartilage injury and miss the last seven games of the season. One player going in the opposite direction was Mickey Forsyth, who joined Notts County for an undisclosed fee after making more than 400 appearances for the Rams.

After losing to Port Vale on 21 February, the Rams collected 19 points from the next 21 and McFarland was First Division Manager of the Month for March. The catalyst for the good run was a televised game against Bolton on 26 February. Goalkeeper Russell Hoult (on loan from Leicester) and 24-year-old striker Lee Mills (£400,000 from Wolves) made their debuts. The Rams won 2-1 and Simon Coleman, now playing for Bolton, sustained a broken leg when challenged by Gabbiadini. Sadly, former Rams favourite Bruce Rioch, now the Bolton manager, had some uncomplimentary things to say about his former club. The recovery from 3-1 down at half-time to win 4-3 at Charlton in January had been sensational, and Paul Simpson had scored a memorable hat-trick in the 3-0 win at home to Portsmouth. But the season's outstanding performance came at promotion-chasing Middlesbrough on 18 March. The Rams raced to a 3-0 half-time lead and conceded two in the second half before Gabbiadini scored the Rams goal of the season to complete a 4-2 victory.

Derby were now eighth but after a 3-3 draw with promotion rivals Wolves at the Baseball Ground, their season died. The run-in saw an excellent 5-0 win against third-placed Tranmere Rovers, but there was too much ground to make up. Two defeats saw the Rams finish ninth and wave goodbye to Roy McFarland who, after spending 27 of the last 28 years working for Derby County, learned that his contract was not being renewed. The fans also said goodbye to the Popular Side terracing. Derby County had to decide whether to build a new home, or develop the Baseball Ground into a 26,000 all-seater stadium. The club spent months in discussion about a new site on Pride Park before, in January 1995, announcing: "The directors of Derby County Football Club have ended 30 months of ground development negotiations by voting to build a new stadium on the site of the current Baseball Ground." And so they demolished a perfectly good pub, the Baseball Hotel, at whose unusually long Victorian bar generations of Rams supporters had enjoyed their pints. Oh, and there was also a new manager of the football club to be appointed.

The Bald Eagle

DERBY COUNTY supporters wondered who their next manager would be. Some of the suggestions flying around the national press were nothing short of alarming – Barry Fry and Osvaldo Ardiles for a start – but most were predictable. Twice the Derby board interviewed Brian Horton, recently sacked by Manchester City where Francis Lee had taken over as chairman. Eventually they appointed Jim Smith – "the "Bald Eagle" – an ordinary player who had proved to be an extraordinarily good manager. Smith had taken both Colchester United and Birmingham City to promotion, Oxford United to the Third and Second Division titles in successive seasons, QPR to a League Cup Final, and Portsmouth to an FA Cup semi-final and the First Division play-offs. He had also been in charge at Blackburn and Newcastle but was working as chief executive of the League Managers' Association when Derby County asked him if he would like to manage again. He jumped at the chance.

Smith's first moves were canny ones. He chose the former Rams midfielder, Steve McClaren, as his first-team coach. He also needed some new players for 1995-96. Three Rams first-team regulars were already on their way out – Craig Short to Everton for £2.65 million, Paul Williams to Coventry City for £1 million, and Mark Pembridge to Sheffield Wednesday for £900,000. Smith used the outgoing transfers to the Rams' advantage, bringing in Everton's 21-year-old centre-half Gary Rowett as a £300,000 makeweight in the Short deal, while Coventry sent the Rams midfielder Sean Flynn as part of the Williams fee. Dutch forward Ron Willems came from Grasshoppers of Zurich for £300,000, midfielder Darryl Powell from Portsmouth for £750,000, and Robbie van der Laan, a midfielder who had the happy knack of bringing out the best in those around him, joined Derby from Port Vale for £700,000). Goalkeeper Russell Hoult's loan was made permanent with £200,000 going to Leicester City.

The major signing of Jim Smith's reign at Derby was still a few weeks away, however, and the Rams were 14th in the table – they had briefly been bottom – and had won only four of their first 14 league matches when they travelled to Tranmere on 4 November 1995. They lost that day, too – 5-1. Their goal came from another debutant, a Croatian centre-half called Igor Stimac, signed for £1.5 million from Hadjuk Split, and just about recovered from a minor road accident caused by him momentarily forgetting that the British drive on the left. Stimac would soon become a cult figure at Derby. When Jim Smith asked him if he played on the right or the left, Stimac had replied: "I can play anywhere." When BBC Radio Derby's Ian Hall, a former Rams forward, asked Stimac how he thought he might become a better player, Stimac looked puzzled. "I don't understand the question," he said.

Supporters saw Stimac not only as the classiest Derby County centre-half since Roy McFarland, but also as a talisman as the Rams won 10 of their next 11 matches. In January, Smith bought Southend United's Chris Powell to Derby, for £800,00. In March, they took their unbeaten run to 20 matches before Sunderland beat them 3-0 at Roker Park. More new players appeared – 20-year-old defender Matt Carbon from Lincoln City, and then centre-forward Ashley Ward, who came from Norwich City for £1 million. On Easter Monday, the Rams got their revenge over Tranmere, Simpson scoring a hat-trick in the 6-2 win at the Baseball Ground. The penultimate match was at home to Crystal Palace. Sunderland were already promoted, the Rams were second with 76 points, Palace third with 75. In only the second minute, the Baseball Ground, bedecked in black and white, erupted when Sturridge put the Rams ahead with his 19th goal of the season. Brown levelled the scores but in the 65th minute the unmarked van der Laan rose to head home Simpson's corner. And that was how it remained. Derby were automatically promoted, a 3-2 defeat at The Hawthorns on the final day of the season didn't matter. "We've got the problem of staying in the Premier League and building a new stadium, which could cost £20 million," Lionel Pickering told reporters. "I read that we will need to spend £20 million on players as well, but I haven't got £20 million. I'm quite confident, though, with the Bosman ruling, that Jim knows the continent and I'm sure he can pull a few more out of the hat."

And indeed he did. On Stimac's recommendation, Smith signed the Croatian international midfielder, Aljosa Asanovic, for £900,00 from

Hadjuk Split. Danish international centre-half Jacob Laursen came from Silkeborg IF, and Christian Dailly, who had played a record 34 times for Scotland under-23s, arrived from Dundee United for £1 million, followed by former England right-back, Paul Parker, on loan from Manchester United. The most important signing, though, was probably that of another former Manchester United player, Paul McGrath, who in October came from Aston Villa for £100,000 and the same again if the Rams avoided relegation. It was a lot to pay for a 36-year-old whose knees were now so dodgy that he was hardly able to train above a gentle amble around the Raynesway ground. But McGrath's skill, experience and mere presence in the back four was invaluable and after they finished 12th, Derby County were happy to pay the second installment on his transfer fee.

The first season in the Premier League produced some memorable moments, not least in only the second home match when a stunning goal from David Beckham was cancelled out by an equally stunning effort from Laursen, who hammered home a free-kick from about the same 30-yard distance to give the Rams a 1-1 draw against Manchester United. Derby's first Premier League win came at Blackburn on 9 September, and there was a run to the FA Cup quarter-finals where the Rams, still trying to shake off a 6-1 league defeat at Middlesbrough, lost 2-0 to Boro at the Baseball Ground as Fabrizio Ravanelli scored his fourth goal against Derby inside a week. Best of all, though, Derby County won 3-2 at Old Trafford where 55,243 saw a wonder goal from the Costa Rican Paulo Wanchope, who had signed along with his Club Sport Heridano teammate, Mauricio Solis, for a joint fee of £1.2 million. Wanchope collected the ball in his own half before running past everyone to beat Peter Schmeichel. At the other end Derby's debutant goalkeeper, Mart Poom, applauded. Poom, already holder of 49 caps for Estonia, had come from Flora Tallinn for £500,00. The same afternoon that the Rams beat United, the Grand National was postponed because of an IRA bomb threat.

Probably the most significant moment of the season, however, came on Sunday, 17 November when Lionel Pickering laid the foundation stone for the new Pride Park Stadium. Derby County were moving after all – the Baseball Hotel had been demolished for nothing. The rain teemed down as Pickering did the honours. Then Igor Stimac said: "Right, now let's beat Middlesbrough!" – which the Rams did, 2-1 at the Baseball Ground, albeit rather fortunately thanks to a Steve Vickers own-goal. The final competitive senior match at the Baseball Ground was staged on 11 May 1997. Arsenal were the visitors and spoiled the party by winning 3-1, even though Tony Adams was sent off. Ashley Ward scored the Rams' last-ever goal on Sir Francis Ley's baseball field.

And so to Friday, 18 July 1997, when Queen Elizabeth II, accompanied by the Duke of Edinburgh, officially opened Derby County's £23 million (eventually £28 million after the north-west corner was developed, raising the stadium's capacity to more than 33,000) new home. Twenty-thousand Rams fans witnessed the occasion, the surviving members of the 1946 FA Cup-winning team were driven around the pitch in a vintage motor-car, and even Mickey Mouse put in an appearance. Two weeks later, the Italian club, Sampdoria, including German international, Jurgen Klinsmann, visited for the official opening game. The crowd for a friendly match was 29,041, and Sampdoria's Vincenzo Montella scored the only goal with a real cracker.

On Wednesday, 13 August came Pride Park's first Premier League game. Or at least that is what should have happened. Wimbledon were the visitors and, 11 minutes into the second half, the Rams led 2-1. But then the floodlights went out. In fact, all the lights went out. After a delay of more than half-an-hour while engineers tried unsuccessfully to restart two failed generators, the referee, Uriah Rennie, abandoned the match. Poor Ashley Ward. He had a unique double – the last goal at the Baseball Ground and the first at Pride Park. Now Pride Park wouldn't count. Rams vice-chairman, Peter Gadsby, said: "We had 11 maintenance people on duty including six electricians but nobody has yet worked out why both generators failed. There was a bang of such strength that it fused them both." After two further games (a Wimbledon home game at Selhurst Park, and a match at Upton Park) suffered the same fate, an investigation was launched over concerns that, while one such event might be accidental, three might be the work of betting syndicates. Ultimately, the incident at Pride Park was deemed to be unconnected with any criminal elements.

Back to the football, the Rams now had a new-look line-up. Meanwhile, Gabbiadini, Ward and Wassall were on their way out of the club – Simpson would follow in November; Asanovic and Carbon in January – but there were tasty new signings. First the elegant Italian international midfielder, Stefano Eranio, arrived from AC Milan on a "Bosman free". Then, after Jim Smith balked at the escalating cost of signing Roberto

Baggio, Eranio suggested striker Francesco Baiano from Fiorentina. So Baiano, capped twice for Italy, joined the Rams for £1.5 million. Both signings were masterstrokes. Although he played behind two strikers, Baiano equalled a Rams record by scoring in six consecutive matches, had 11 by Christmas and was voted the supporters' Player of the Year for 1997-98, albeit he was never as effective thereafter. Eranio just oozed class, whether he was in midfield or used as a wing-back. His control and passing were a delight to watch. So, with another £1 million striker in Jamaican international Deon Burton from Portsmouth, the Rams looked set for a good season, during which further new signings were made. They included Rory Delap from Carlisle United, and Lars Bohinen, winner of 49 Norway caps, for whom the Rams paid Blackburn Rovers £1.7 million. Bohinen was to achieve relatively little at Derby County, a club he would occasionally criticise on his website, hardly a good career move.

Pride Park highlights included a 4-0 win over Southampton in September, a 2-2 draw with Manchester United in October, and a 3-0 thumping of Arsenal in November. The week after they beat Arsenal, the Rams were involved in an astonishing game at Elland Road where they were 3-0 up after 15 minutes but lost 4-3. Many Derby fans, caught in very heavy traffic on the M1, didn't arrive until their team had scored all its goals. It was Leeds who inflicted upon the Rams their worst home result of the season when, in mid-March, the Elland Road team put five goals past Derby without reply. Late April could have seen an even worse result. After 15 minutes, the Rams trailed 4-0 to Leicester City at Pride Park. After the fourth goal went in, there was a clatter of seats as hundreds, if not thousands, of home fans left the ground in disgust. They missed a spirited performance by the Rams who, while their cause was lost, battled to ensure that it became no worse. The season ended on a high note with a 1-0 home win over third-placed Liverpool in front of a Pride Park record 30,492 fans. Wanchope netted his 13th league goal, which made him Derby County's leading scorer of the season. Wanchope was a remarkable player who scored some remarkable goals, one of them, against Blackburn in January, appearing to bounce off every part of his body before ending up in the net.

The Rams finished 1997-98 in ninth, two points below Aston Villa who claimed the final UEFA Cup place, and in 1998-99 they went one better. Before the season started, Derby broke their club record fee again, this time for the Argentinean defender, Horacio Carbonari, who cost £2.7 million from Rosario Central. His Italian roots meant that there was no restriction on him as a non-EU player. Carbonari arrived with a reputation as a taker of fierce free-kicks, which had apparently earned him the nickname of "the Bazooka", although another version is that this was a childhood nickname linked to a circus dwarf of the same name that he had befriended as a boy. Also coming in was another "Bosman free", German left-back, Stefan Schnoor, veteran of 131 Bundesliga games for Hamburg. Schnoor would replace Chris Powell, who had inexplicably been allowed to join Charlton Athletic. Powell didn't want to leave. Rams fans didn't want him to leave. Derby County have never replaced him. It didn't make sense.

But, even without Chris Powell, the Rams were about to embark upon their most successful season in recent times. In the summer, no less than five Derby players had been involved in the France World Cup, albeit with contrasting fortunes. Christian Dailly's Scotland, and Deon Burton's and Darryl Powell's Jamaica, failed to get past the first group stage. Denmark reached the quarter-finals but Jacob Laursen had been restricted to only half a game. Igor Stimac, though, had been a star of the Croatian team (that also included Aljosa Asanovic) unluckily beaten in the semi-final by the host nation. Dailly was to play only one more game for the Rams. In August he was transferred to Blackburn Rovers for £5.3 million, easily the biggest fee that Derby County had ever received.

Six matches into the season, the Rams, with a team that played exciting, attractive football, stood second in the Premier League. Then they lost 1-0 at Aston Villa, followed immediately by defeats at the hands of Spurs and Newcastle. The pinnacle had been reached and the Rams now started to fall. Not too far, though. They ended the season in eighth position, again narrowly missing a place in the UEFA Cup. There was a Premier League double over Liverpool and a narrow FA Cup quarter-final defeat at Highbury. Rams fans always travelled with optimism. On its day, this Derby team could beat anyone, although towards the end of the season there were unsettling reverses at Leeds (4-1) and West Ham (5-1).

In February, Jim Smith had lost his first-team coach when Steve McClaren was tempted away by Alex Ferguson who wanted McClaren as his new assistant at Old Trafford. It left the Derby manager somewhat exposed. McClaren was acknowledged as one of the most innovative coaches in the game. Smith replaced him with such respected men as Ray

Harford and Malcolm Crosby. But an ideal management partnership had been broken up.

In July 1999, Paolo Wanchope was transferred to West Ham United. The move made sense. It was wiser to accept £3.5 million than risk a free transfer at the end of the player's contract a year later. Stimac was unsettled and a month later, he also went to Upton Park, although he would soon return to Croatia where he had business interests. In November, with Smith now having to reshape the team to deal with what had turned into a relegation battle, Baiano was released to a Serie B club. And just before the March 2000 transfer deadline, Spencer Prior, the centre-half signed from Leicester to replace Christian Dailly, went off to help Manchester City into the Premier League.

The Rams tried to buy way out of trouble with the signings – for £3 million each – of Craig Burley from Celtic, Branko Strupar from the Belgian club, KRC Genk, and Georgiou Kinkladze from Ajax Amsterdam. Scotland midfielder Burley was the most successful for Derby. Strupar, Croatian by birth but a Belgium international, was a proven goalscorer but dogged by injury at Pride Park. The fans loved Kinkladze but he needed several weeks to get match fit and, as skilful as he was, wasn't really the man you wanted beside you in the trenches.

Esteban Fuertes was a particularly interesting addition to Derby County's playing staff in 1999. Signed from Colón de Santa Fe of Argentina for £2.3 million, Fuertes scored twice in 10 games, was sent off at Bradford City, and then wasn't allowed back in the UK after a Rams midweek break in Portugal. Apparently, the question "Well, how much does an Italian passport cost then?" had been key to him signing for the Rams. Far less complicated were the incoming transfers of Seth Johnson (from Crewe Alexandra for £3 million) and 19-year-old Lee Morris (Sheffield United, £2 million rising with appearances).

But despite all the big-money signings, the 1999-2000 season proved uncomfortable viewing. In contrast to the previous season, the Rams had to wait until their fifth game before registering their first points. A 5-0 Pride Park drubbing at the hands of newly promoted Sunderland in mid-September was in stark contrast to the 3-1 home win over Chelsea six weeks later. On the whole, however, there were too many narrow defeats and the Rams managed only 38 points to finish 16th.

By the end of 2000-01 it was down to 17th. Early on the Rams were bottom of the table. Then, in November, Smith signed the Nigerian international centre-half, Taribo West, from Milan. West was a free agent – and a free spirit. Every time the player went off to play for his country, or to attend to the church he had founded in Milan, Jim Smith never knew quite when to expect him back at Raynesway. But West played enough times, and with enough authority, to stabilise the Rams' defence, helping to steady Derby-born youngster, Chris Riggott, and former Manchester United junior, Danny Higginbotham. The Rams guaranteed their safety in their penultimate game with an improbable 1-0 win at Old Trafford against the already-crowned champions. The goal was a spectacular one from Malcolm Christie, who had signed in March 1998 from Nuneaton Borough and soon found himself playing in the Premier League and winning England under-21 international caps. He finished this season leading score with 12 in all games. In July, Rory Delap was sold to Southampton for £4 million as Derby County raised some money in a deteriorating financial situation.

On 7 October 2001, Derby County sacked Jim Smith. The season had started well – a 2-1 home win over Blackburn Rovers, a game ignited on the stroke of half-time by a spectacular goal from Fabrizio Ravanelli, signed from Lazio just before the start of the season. The "White Feather" performed his trademark celebration – pulling his shirt over his head and then racing around the pitch, arms outstretched – while Derby supporters still wondered if Ravanelli was really worth £40,000-a-week. Probably not. It would be mid-November before the Rams won another league match, by which time they were bottom of the Premier League.

There were some bad days at Pride Park in 2001-02, none more so than on 15 September. Leicester City were the visitors. It was four days after the terrible events of 9/11 when terrorists flew two airliners into the twin towers of New York's World Trade Center, killing 2,996 people. In the aftermath of the week's shocking events, the mood in the ground was sombre. An unseasonable wind swirled and gusted, spoiling play. And the long-standing rivalry between the clubs gave the game an extra edge. But nothing could have prepared fans for the way the match would end – with controversial Leicester midfielder Robbie Savage needing a police escort at the final whistle.

In the fourth minute, fed by the efforts of Kinkladze and Ravanelli, the Rams went ahead through Deon Burton. After 30 minutes Derby old boy Dean Sturridge equalised. Early in the game Savage and Seth Johnson had both been booked after Johnson was adjudged to have fouled the Leicester man, while the latter was cautioned for squaring up to Johnson. It was a confrontation that was to rumble on. Meanwhile both goalkeepers found themselves under continued pressure as the teams battled it out in an exciting, if rather scrappy, game. Sturridge scored his second, and after Burton was bundled over by Marshall, Ravanelli put away the equalising penalty, only for it all to come to a controversial end when the Foxes earned a last-minute penalty when Savage appeared to dive dramatically after an innocuous looking tackle from Higginbotham. Muzzy Izzet converted the spot kick. In fairness to the Rams fans, it was as much the manner of Savage's "victory celebration" upon winning the penalty that incensed them.

Indeed, he made the *Observer* newspaper's "best 10 dives in football history" feature: "Robbie makes it so high in the list for sheer effort: a corrosive 90 minutes, a last-minute dive in the area, a hopeful look to the referee and a fist-pumping explosion in front of the home fans. Derby players chased him all the way to the corner flag, then tried to mug him in the tunnel afterwards. 'We've seen players for years who are very clever at diving for penalties,' said Derby boss Jim Smith, 'but he's not very clever and his penalties become riots. It's always him.' Robbie said: 'I've never dived in my career. I was blameless.'"

Three weeks later, with the Rams next to bottom – Ravanelli still seemed able to score in every match but now Derby couldn't win even one of them – Jim Smith paid with his job. The season was only seven games old. Some supporters felt that it was a ludicrous decision by the Derby board. Others argued that Smith had been allowed to carry for too long. Whichever, Derby County were in a mess.

Managers' Merry-go-Round

O N 16 March 2002, Derby County beat Bolton Wanderers 3-1 at the Reebok Stadium. The result didn't change anything – Bolton were still 18th, Derby still 19th – but so poor were the Trotters, and so bright were the Rams, that thousands of away fans left the ground believing that the season could be salvaged. "Can't see Bolton winning another game," they said as they made for their trains, coaches and cars. But Bolton won their next two matches, Derby lost their next seven and, with two matches still to play, the Rams' relegation was confirmed with a defeat at Anfield.

It wasn't surprising that a team that had three managers in the same season should be demoted. After the board sacked Jim Smith in October – Stefano Eranio was so distressed at Smith's departure that he asked to be released immediately from his contract – they appointed his assistant, Colin Todd, to replace him. Todd had been a fine Derby player, one of the best in the club's history, but his appointment as manager did nothing to excite supporters. He had managed Middlesbrough and Bolton before taking over at Swindon, which is where he'd been for six months when Derby approached him to become Smith's assistant. Swindon were annoyed, and Todd was suspended until compensation was agreed. Now Smith was offered the post of director of football at Derby. But Todd didn't want him around the training ground. The parting was less than amicable.

After completing the £7 million transfer of Seth Johnson to Leeds United – a deal set in motion by Smith – for some reason Todd began to spend the money in France, bringing in Pierre Ducrocq on loan, François Grenet and Luciano Zavagno, none of whom were going to rescue Derby County. Neither was the much-travelled Benito Carbone, who cash-strapped Bradford City were mightily relieved to unload. Todd presented a forlorn figure on the Pride Park touchline, and after the Rams were knocked out of the FA Cup by next-to-bottom of the Third Division Bristol Rovers, he too was sacked. Todd had been in charge for only 15 Premier League games. His going so soon was tantamount to an open admission by the Rams board that they should never have appointed him in the first place.

So by mid-January, Derby County were on their third manager of the season. A few days after he had become the latest Aston Villa manager to develop a strained relationship with Villa chairman, "Deadly" Doug Ellis, former Rams playing favourite, John Gregory, returned to Derby. Gregory immediately signed Rob Lee and Warren Barton from Newcastle United, and when the Rams won at the Reebok on that mid-March day, he had edged them towards possible survival. But that was far as the recovery went. With an appalling record of 24 defeats, Derby went down with Leicester.

There was to be no quick return. In fact, things got worse. The Rams ended 2002-03 in 18th place in Division One. And they had yet another new manager. In March, Gregory was suspended for "gross misconduct", allegations that were unspecified and unproven. It was one of the shabbiest episodes in the club's history. Gregory was dismissed, made a claim for damages against Derby County, and in April 2004 agreed an out-of-court settlement with a new board after Lionel Pickering had stood down as chairman.

In the meantime – apparently driven by one Fred Vinton, the Derby director appointed by investors Electra Fleming – former Ipswich Town manager George Burley found himself as Derby County's "interim manager" for the remainder of 2002-03. Many players had departed: Poom to Sunderland; Higginbotham to Southampton; Riggott and Christie to Middlesbrough (for much less than their value, thanks to the Rams dallying as the transfer market collapsed); Burton back to Portsmouth; Darryl Powell who was released but later signed for Birmingham City; and Carbonari back to Argentina.

Three loan signings – Paul Ritchie from Manchester City, Tommy Mooney from Birmingham City and Nick Chadwick from Everton – were the only incomers of note. When Burley arrived, the Rams were 20th and had lost six of their last nine matches. He took charge for the last seven games, from which the Rams earned the nine points that took them clear of relegation.

It was enough for Burley to be appointed full-time – but with instructions to reduce the wage bill. So out went his nephew, Craig Burley (who had been sidelined for a long spell due to injury), Kinkladze and Ravanelli, although for some time to come the Rams were apparently still paying the White Feather's huge salary. With no money for even moderate signings, in 2003-04, Burley had to work with free transfers and loans. One of the more successful frees was Birmingham City centre-half Michael Johnson who, like the Portuguese midfielder Candido Costa, on loan from Porto, played the entire season. Other loanees, like Matthias Svensson (Charlton) and Leon Osman (Everton) arrived on shorter-term deals. Osman was a huge influence on the Rams staying up, and at the end of the season the new Rams board said that they were trying to sign him permanently. Most supporters didn't believe that for a moment.

Academy players Lee Holmes, Lee Grant, Tom Huddlestone and Marcus Tudgay made the leap into the first team. The Brazilian forward, Junior – who'd scored a hat-trick against Derby for Walsall the previous season – also made a promising start but after scoring at the City Ground in late September, he injured cruciate ligaments in the same match and was out for seven months. In March, Canadian international, Paul Peschisolido, was signed on a free transfer from Sheffield United, and scored four times in his 11 games. It was always going to be an uphill battle and relegation wasn't avoided until the penultimate game, and by only one point.

Those Three Amigos

While on-field activities continued to test the patience of the faithful, matters at boardroom level were even more turbulent. For some time, Derby County had been struggling financially, mainly due to some poor decisions in the transfer market. Immediately after relegation, Lionel Pickering had refused bids for Rams players totalling £12 million at a time when the club's debt to the Co-operative Bank stood at £15 million. The owner felt that the players who had taken the Rams down could get them up again. Supporters weren't so sure. The man who at one time been had been, quite rightly, hailed a hero by Rams fans now alienated them by suggesting something that most regarded as nothing short of diabolical –

Forest were made mugs by a coffee cup

WHEN Nottingham Forest arrived at Pride Park on 20 March 2004 there was more at stake than just bragging rights until the next "A52" derby game. Both the Rams and Forest were in trouble at the wrong end of the Championship. And when the Rams stormed into a 3-0 lead after only 37 minutes, Derby supporters drooled over the prospect of sheer humiliation for their fiercest rivals. But even they couldn't have imagined the farce that left Forest's faces as red as their shirts.

The Rams' storming start brought goals from skipper Ian Taylor, and two from Paul Peschisolido, who took his tally to four in three games following his arrival from Sheffield United 10 days earlier.

After Taylor had given the Rams a fourth-minute lead – a superb finish from Peschisolido's through ball – Peschisolido himself made it 2-0 in the 26th minute. But what a daft goal it was.

It was a windy afternoon with litter blowing across the pitch as Forest's Republic of Ireland under-21 international goalkeeper, Barry Roche, sliced an attempted clearance straight into the path of Peschisolido, who had the easiest of tasks to tap the ball into an empty net.

What had gone wrong? Well, Wes Morgan's back-pass was straightforward enough – until it struck an empty disposable coffee cup that had been blown into Roche's penalty area. It was a goal that would go down in the folklore of this always bitterly fought fixture.

Before half-time Peschisolido had scored again, this time a well-constructed goal after the Canadian international had exchanged passes with Marcus Tudgay.

Either side of half-time Forest pulled back with goals from Gareth Taylor and Gareth Williams. Michael Johnson did not cut out Matthieu Louis-Jean's cross and Taylor scored a brave goal from close range. Before the interval, Gareth Taylor's header hit the Derby crossbar and, after the break, Williams forced home a rebound to set up a nerve-jangling finish.

But Derby sealed the result nine minutes from the end when Tudgay's deflected shot from the edge of the penalty area completely wrong-footed Roche to complete for him what had been a day of great misfortune.

The coffee cup incident provided great copy for journalists: " ... Derby will be looking to get a sponsorship deal with Kenco, the manufacturers of the drink that will do little to cure Joe Kinnear's hangover after this damaging defeat ... It is hard not to feel sorry for Roche, who will find it hard to drink coffee again after the horrendous encounter with the plastic cup ... " wrote the *Daily Mirror*'s Ian Taylor.

Peschisolido said afterwards: "I felt really sorry for the keeper. It must have bobbled up as he hit it and he shinned it to me. I turned, expecting him to have the ball, and there it was in front of me – so I stuck it in the net."

if they didn't like what was going on, then they should head down the A52 to watch Nottingham Forest instead.

There was talk of the involvement of former Coventry City chairman, Bryan Richardson, and a notional £30 million bond. Instead Derby County were forced into temporary receivership. Pickering was removed from the board and, seemingly out of nowhere, a new board appeared, comprising barrister and deputy coroner for North Yorkshire, John Sleightholme, marketing consultant Steve Harding, and Jeremy Keith who described himself as a "business strategist". They were the public face of a consortium that had apparently come up with £15 million to restructure loans from the Co-operative Bank, which was now owed £26 million. None of them had any obvious connections to the city, let alone to Derby County, but they assured a packed press conference that they were football fans "in the broadest sense". But who, actually, were the investors? Sleightholme said simply: "We were enabled to arrange finance through a group of investors who wish to remain anonymous but wish to support the current board and Derby County." Brian Clough was among those unconvinced. "I can't see how they can remain anonymous forever," he told the *Derby Evening Telegraph*. "They'll have to be named when the club's signed over to the new chairman and there's also the question of fans having a right to know who's making decisions about their club." Sadly, Brian Clough had not long to live. In September 2004, the great Derby County legend died from stomach cancer. He was 69.

Despite being severely hamstrung in 2004-05 – there was no money to spend on new players, and the £6.4m wage bill would have to be "considered" – George Burley transformed Derby County from relegation candidates to play-off semi-finalists in what had now been rebranded the "Football League Championship". His most significant signings were Spanish midfielder Iñigo Idiakez, who came on a free transfer from Madrid's Rayo Vallecano, and Polish striker Grzegorz Rasiak, on a free transfer from Italian club, AC Sienna. In November, Burley signed striker Tommy Smith, whose contract talks with Sunderland had stalled.

At last Rams fans had something to celebrate. They voted Idiakez their Player of the Year, Rasiak was leading scorer with 16 league goals, and Smith scored 11 as Derby finished fourth with a settled team – a squad of only 24 players and seven of them played 10 games or less.

In the second half of the season, the Rams had lost only six times in 24 games, including one run of only one defeat in 14 games, They also equalled the club record for away wins in a season – 12 – and set a new record of six consecutive away victories. But injuries to both Rasiak and Idiakez saw them enter the play-offs under strength and they were unable to overturn a 2-0 defeat in the away leg against Billy Davies's Preston North End. From the supporters' point of view, though, it had been the most enjoyable season for some years.

Behind the scenes, however, there was a festering atmosphere. George Burley had fallen out with Murdo Mackay, a football agent and a man with several failed business enterprises behind him. It now appeared that Mackay had been deeply involved in the takeover. At first Mackay's role at Derby was unspecified but then he began to appear at the Moor Farm training ground, resplendent in monogrammed tracksuit. He was the club's new director of football. It was all too much for Burley, who saw his managerial territory invaded, especially when, in January 2005, without speaking to the manager, Mackay brokered the transfer of 18-year-old Tom Huddlestone to Spurs (who also signed Rasiak after the Rams failed to win promotion). Burley had also been the target of scurrilous, all unsubstantiated, rumours about his private life. He dealt with it with dignity and at the end of the season he left Derby County. Despite a successful season, the club's debt had now reached £30 million, and fans were dismayed when a refinancing scheme saw Pride Park sold to the Panama-based ABC Corporation to which the club were to pay £1 million per year in rent.

Derby County started 2005-06 with their fifth manager in four years. Phil Brown, veteran of more than 600 appearances as a defender in the lower leagues, had been Sam Allardyce's assistant and then caretaker boss at Bolton Wanderers. Derby County was his first permanent appointment in football management – if there is such a thing as permanency in that profession. Unfortunately, Brown was unable to maintain the momentum and form that Burley had found, although in fairness almost anyone would have struggled in having to work for one of the worst boards in football. But Brown did himself no favours with supporters. "The way they questioned my decisions was absolutely disgraceful", he complained to BBC Radio Derby after fans booed his substitution of their favourite, Paul Peschisolido. It showed a complete misunderstanding of the relationship between lifelong supporters and here-today-gone-tomorrow owners, managers and players. In early January, in an attempt to distance himself from the repeated failures of his team, Brown again spoke to

Radio Derby: "At this moment in time, it's pointing in the direction that the players aren't good enough to be able to (1) take on the instructions that we give them and (2) deal with the situation when the pressure is turned up. And it's disappointing. Okay, there's a disappointing group of players in there but you keep on shooting yourself in the foot week in and week out. Something has to change."

And change it did. After a 6-1 battering by Coventry City in the league and a 3-1 defeat in the third round of the FA Cup by League One high-flyers, Colchester United, the Rams found themselves in a precarious 19th place in the table, and with nothing to fight for save what seemed sure to be a long, hard relegation battle, Brown was relieved of his duties. One of his last acts had been to sign West Brom centre-half, Darren Moore, for a fee of £300,000, rising to £500,000 depending on appearances. Moore would become a towering figure in the Rams defence, so Brown had done the Rams at least one good turn.

Instead of installing a new permanent manager, the board elected to place the club's Academy manager, Terry Westley, in a caretaker role until the end of the season. Westley's first five games in charge saw no wins, but form gradually improved and, eventually, so did results, confirming the Rams' continued Championship status. Westley clearly wanted the job permanently. Speaking to BBC Radio Derby's Alex Trelinski, he said: "Being inside the club and working with the players, I'm aware more than anyone else – certainly from outside the football club – what is required to take the team forward. I know people say it'd be a big blow to the academy if I left that job, but it's no good having a great academy if we get relegated. The only way the academy can thrive is if we get back to the Premiership – and if I could be the person involved in taking them there, I'd be only too delighted. But the new manager needs to be put in place quickly because there are players out there and from 1 May we can start buying again." Westley, though, wouldn't be at Pride Park to buy anyone. He wasn't offered the job and turned down a chance to return to his Academy duties.

None of the directors who had appointed Brown were at Pride Park, either. Early in 2006 there surfaced disagreement between chairman John Sleightholme and chief executive Jeremy Keith. In April, Sleightholme resigned: "My position has been made untenable. Recently it has come to my attention that meetings have been held, important decisions taken and documents signed without my knowledge. Important information has been withheld from me." Later that month a consortium of businessmen, led by Peter Gadsby, took Derby County into local ownership once more.

The saga of the "Three Amigos", as the previous board had been dubbed, wasn't over, though. In March 2009, a jury at Northampton Crown Court was told that following the takeover of Derby County, for just £3, Jeremy Keith, Murdo Mackay, and Andrew Mackenzie, the club's finance director, had each been paid £125,000 plus VAT by the club, which was not approved by the board. After being found guilty of conspiracy to defraud the club, Mackenzie and Mackay were each sentenced to three years' imprisonment. Keith was sentenced to 18 months, having been convicted of false accounting. A Monaco-based lawyer, David Lowe, was jailed for two years after being convicted of money laundering. The court heard that Lowe, the legal adviser during the takeover, had received £81,895 for part of Mackenzie's share of the commissions, and channelled it to Mackenzie via one of Lowe's companies registered in the Isle of Man. Keith was also disqualified from being a company director for three years, while Mackenzie and Mackay were both disqualified for five years. There has never been any suggestion that Sleightholme or Harding had in any way been involved.

The judge, Ian Alexander QC, described the fraud as "in some ways more reprehensible" than usual. Derby County supporters wouldn't argue with that.

An Unexpected Promotion

ERBY COUNTY'S new manager was in a position that none of his immediate predecessors had enjoyed – he was able to dip into the transfer market. In June 2006, Billy Davies, recently manager of Preston North End, was helicoptered into the Moor Farm training complex to tell the waiting press: "I felt it was time to move on to a fresh challenge. I had four great years at Preston. There will be some people disappointed to see me go – there will be some people happy to see me go." Which camp his former chairman, Derek Shaw, fell into wasn't clear. Shaw had tried to hold on to Davies but eventually agreed a compensation package with Derby after the two men hadn't spoken to each other for several days.

With the Rams now financially more stable, Davies was able to sign centre-forward Steve Howard from Luton Town – Derby's first £1 million signing for some years – who quickly proved a great favourite. He was joined at Pride Park by goalkeeper Stephen Bywater, from West Ham United for £225,00, and defender Dean Leacock, from Fulham for £375,000. Midfielder Matt Oakley, veteran of more than 250 games for Southampton, including the 2003 FA Cup Final, was appointed team captain. However, the season did not get off to the best start – only five points from the first six matches – and with the departure, before the end of August, of Iñigo Idiakez and Tommy Smith, fans wondered what lay ahead. But then a 1-0 win at Wolves in mid-September was the key to a dramatic turnaround in the Rams' fortunes. Although their successes never seemed emphatic, Derby lost only four of the next 27 matches. They won all six in November, and between the end of December and mid-February an eight-match-winning streak that included six league games and two FA Cup ties, took the Rams six points clear at the top of the Championship.

Throughout the season Davies again went into the transfer market: right-back Tyrone Mears on loan from West Ham, signing permanently for £1 million at the end of the season; left-back Jay McEveley from Blackburn Rovers for £600,000; winger Gary Teale from Wigan Athletic for £600,00; midfielder Stephen Pearson from Celtic for £750,000; midfielder David Jones, a former "Fergie fledgling" at Manchester United, initially on loan. And Seth Johnson, plagued by injury at Leeds, returned to Pride Park. However, following their exit from the fifth round of the FA Cup at Plymouth, the Rams began to wobble. With only six points from their next five games they slipped down the table, although former trainee, Giles Barnes, was voted Championship Player of the Month for March. In a season that saw the Rams win by a two-goal margin or more on only six occasions, even a 5-1 win over Colchester couldn't stop the slide, and with only 15 points from their next 10 games, Derby fell out of the automatic promotion places, their focus shifting to making the play-offs. That they managed in comfort with a third-place finish.

The play-off semi-final games against Southampton proved tense affairs and featured two former Rams players in Idiakez and Rasiak, and former Derby boss, George Burley. After the first leg, Derby led 2-1, but on a night of torrential rain at Pride Park a crowd of 31,569 saw Southampton win the second leg 3-2 with a last-minute Rasiak goal, leaving the teams level 4-4 on aggregate. Penalties! Leon Best (who had already scored an own-goal) fired Southampton's first spot-kick wide. Jones, Howard, Barnes and McEveley all scored theirs for Derby. Southampton kept in touch. Then Idiakez stepped up. You could probably have heard the proverbial pin drop. All that changed when he shot high and wide to propel his former employers to the Final.

"It will be an unbelievable day out and we will go with great belief we can go all the way," said Billy Davies. Rams fans believed him and on 28 May 2007, tens of thousands of them made the trip to the rebuilt Wembley Stadium. For Derby it was a match that mirrored much of the season that had gone before – the nervous Rams somehow managing to keep out opponents that had enjoyed much of the possession. In the end the teams were separated by a single goal – scored in the 61st minute by Stephen Pearson. It was the first of his Derby career. For Rams fans the last 29 minutes seemed like an eternity. Numerous bookings were awarded and free-kicks conceded. Then referee Graham Poll, in what was his last professional refereeing task, sounded the final whistle to confirm that Derby County were back in the Premier League.

It had been far from a classic, but few Rams fans could be heard complaining. It was reckoned that, thanks largely to Sky Television money, the win was worth £52 million – the largest reward for any single match in world football. The national press, however, were less inclined to overlook the game's inadequacies. *The Guardian*: "Not since the Brink's-Mat robbery at Heathrow in 1983 has such a phenomenal sum been purloined so inappropriately."

It had indeed been an unexpected achievement and, alongside the optimism, supporters feared that the success might have come too soon. Billy Davies's post-match interviews seemed to hint that he thought so too. On the Wembley pitch, moments after the final whistle, when asked what it was like to be a Premier League manager Davies would say only: "Well, we'll enjoy the night …" before going to take the congratulations of one of his directors. Later, when asked about his reticence, Davies said: "I don't think there's anything guaranteed 100 per cent in life. I want to have discussions for sure and there's lots of talking to be done. I'm not saying I don't want to be Derby manager, I'm saying that I don't think in life anything is 100 per cent guaranteed. Now we'll sit down, have a chat and see what happens. I'm not prepared to discuss it at the moment and I'm not prepared to go into specifics. I've never said I'm leaving but it was always my intention to get to the end of the season and have a discussion."

Worst Team in History?

Davies, however, was still at Pride Park at the beginning of 2007-08, overseeing major changes in the playing staff. Out went goalkeepers Lee Grant and Lee Camp, defender Paul Boertien, and midfielder Morten Bisgaard. The play-off Final had also been Seth Johnson's last appearance for Derby County. In came strikers Robert Earnshaw (£3 million from Norwich City) and Kenny Miller (Celtic, £2.25 million), and defenders Andy Todd (son of Colin, £750,000 from Blackburn Rovers), and Claude Davis (£3 million from Sheffield United).

After a 2-2 draw at home to Portsmouth on the opening day, and a narrow defeat at Manchester City, maybe things didn't look too bad. But then it became all too obvious that this Derby County team, promoted almost accidentally, was way out of its depth. There was a 6-0 thrashing at Liverpool, three weeks after that a 5-0 defeat at Arsenal, and a 5-0 home defeat by West Ham. A fortnight later, Chelsea won 2-0 at Pride Park. It was 24 November; the Rams had only five points from 14 games, had scored only five goals, conceded 33, and were bottom of the Premier League.

In the after-match press conference, Billy Davies decided to go on the offensive: "It would be nice if I could have five minutes with him [Adam Pearson, the Rams new chairman]. But I can't, he is a very busy man. I haven't spoken to him for two or three weeks." That ensured that the two did speak, first thing on Monday morning. There could be only one outcome: "We have decided mutually in the best interest of both parties that to go our separate ways is the correct decision at this time," said Pearson.

Pearson – who had come from Hull City to work on attracting new investment to the Rams – told BBC Radio Derby: "I was surprised on Saturday night when it was suggested I hadn't spoken to Billy for three weeks because that is totally inaccurate. My last formal meeting 10 days ago was to ask for a list of players for Christmas and there have been subsequent phone calls, so that caused a little bit of tension. Things were brought to a head because there were continual comments about lack of investment, and that's hard for this club to accept because the wage bill's been increased significantly, £12m has been spent on players, and the debt has been reduced by £6m." In other words the board had lost patience with the manager because of his negative comments.

Davies had certainly worked wonders in getting the Rams promoted. His teams were always difficult to beat at Championship level, always awkward, fight-to-the-finish opponents. Squeezing through via the play-offs had left less time to plan, although shouldn't there have been a Plan A and a Plan B, just in case? And hadn't Davies had money to spend, and hadn't some of his bigger deals disappointed? Claude Davis was later dubbed "the worst major signing in Derby County's history". But now Billy Davies was gone – and without a relegation on his CV. That dubious honour fell to Paul Jewell, who had resigned as Wigan Athletic manager after taking the Latics into the Premier League at the end of the previous season. Jewell appeared unable to do anything to check Derby's embarrassing, crashing tumble, despite bringing in several players including Danny Mills on loan from Manchester City, former Manchester United goalkeeper Roy Carroll on a free transfer from Rangers, and centre-half Alan Stubbs on a free from Everton. Most controversial of all, he signed Robbie Savage from Blackburn Rovers for £1.5 million. Savage had baggage with most clubs, but especially with Derby fans still smarting at his spectacular celebration after winning a penalty at Pride Park six years earlier. To his credit, Savage publicly acknowledged that, and set about winning over supporters, which he did with plenty of credit to spare.

But he couldn't help Derby avoid the inevitable. When the Rams faced Bolton Wanderers on 2 January 2008, they were 10 points from safety. Skipper Matt Oakley declared that they had to win at the Reebok, "otherwise the season's over". Derby lost 1-0. Eight days later, Oakley was transferred to Leicester City for £500,000, a week after Steve Howard had moved to the same club for £1.25 million. Months later, Rams fans were still chuntering about letting Oakley go.

Jewell's 16th game as Derby County manager was on 23 February 2008 against his former club, Wigan. A 2–0 defeat set a Derby club record of 21 league games without victory. On 29 March a 2-2 draw with Fulham confirmed the Rams' relegation as the first club in Premier League history to be doomed before the beginning of April. Derby County went into the record books for a number of other reasons, too. They won only one game all season – that under Jewell's predecessor – which meant that they shared a 108-year-old record with Loughborough FC. And they finished with only 11 points, an all-time low. The last three home matches heaped humiliation upon misery: lost 6-0 to Aston Villa, 6-2 to Arsenal, and 4-0 to Reading.

One victory, eight draws, 29 defeats, and a goal-difference of minus 69 (20 scored, 89 conceded) – Derby County new owners, General Sports and Entertainment (GSE), must have wondered what they had bought in January 2008. What did the Americans hope to get out of their involvement at Pride Park? The obvious answer is – ultimately, a profit. Like every business, that is what GSE is about. In 1998, for instance, it bought the Fort Wayne Wizards, a minor league baseball club that had experienced seven straight years of decline. Apathy was the biggest commodity it had to offer. GSE turned it around before, in 2006, selling to Hardball Capital, an Atlanta-based company that invests in baseball-related businesses. The Fort Wayne franchise (renamed the TinCaps) continued to set records and shatter attendances in its Midwest League. Could GSE do the same for Derby County?

Not in the short term. The Rams' drop back into the Championship saw further decline, even though Jewell guided them to their first League Cup semi-final in 40 years. Summer signings included defender Paul Connolly (Plymouth Argyle), midfielders Kris Commons (Forest), Steve Davies (Tranmere Rovers) and Paul Green (Doncaster Rovers), and centre-forward Rob Hulse, from Sheffield United for £1.75 million. Out went Earnshaw (to Forest for £3.5 million), Miller (to Rangers for £2 million), Craig Fagan (back to Hull City, £750,000), Jones (Wolves for £1.2 million), Moore, Edworthy and Johnson. In August, without his manager's permission, Tyrone Mears took it upon himself to fly to France to have a trial with Olympique de Marseille. Mears was fined six weeks' wages, but with him determined to leave and Jewell declaring that the defender would never again play for the club while he was in charge, the Rams had little choice but to agree to the player going on a season-long loan to the French club.

Jewell's first victory as Derby manager came in the second game of 2008-09 when a hat-trick by Nathan Ellington, on a season-long loan from Watford, helped beat Lincoln City after extra-time in the first round of the League Cup. Derby went all the way to the semi-final where they lost 4-3 on aggregate to the eventual winners, Manchester United. The Rams also lost to United in the FA Cup, 4-1 at home in the fifth round. But it was Derby's Championship form that really mattered. On 14 September 2008, Paul Jewell finally won a league game for Derby County, 2-1 at home to Sheffield United. He had been in charge for almost a year.

Meanwhile, the club's new owners had announced that the Rams' debt now stood at £25 million, some £6 million less than when they took over. The intention was to reduce it by another £10 million over the next year, leaving only the £15 million mortgage on Pride Park. If fans were encouraged by this news, they were soon having to absorb the fact that most of the so-called "parachute payment" from the relegation season had already been spent on players. Supporters were also warned that the club needed to reduce the annual wage bill by more than £2.5 million. And then there was the question – still being asked in 2013 – as to who actually did own the club. Adam Pearson, Derby's chairman when the deal was done, said that GSE's president, Andy Appleby, now owned 93 per cent "on behalf of GSE". However, Appleby explained that "GSE will be managing the investment of members of the USA consortium they have brought together". GSE, it appeared, was simply managing the club on behalf of the investment group, but neither Appleby, now Derby County's chairman, nor Tom Glick, the club's new chief executive, could reveal the identities of members of that consortium. "We cannot say at this time. It is not a matter of secrecy. GSE has a number of investors and they are not interested in a public role," said Glick.

In November, for the first time in three years the Rams faced an East Midlands derby against Nottingham Forest. The game was to prove controversial. It ended 1-1, but only after referee Stuart Attwell had disallowed two Derby goals in the final minutes. Attwell also booked eight players and sent off the Reds' midfielder Lewis McGugan. Paul Jewell echoed the fans' fury, accusing Attwell of "losing control" of the game and "robbing" his team of a victory. It seemed at least some of those in charge agreed; Attwell, a young referee who had been "fast-tracked", was missing from the following week's roster.

When they lost 1-0 at home to Ipswich Town on 28 December, the Rams were 18th in the Championship. Paul Jewell had long looked like a manager running out of ideas, inspiration and even interest. It would be his last game in charge of Derby County.

A Man Named Clough

DERBY COUNTY once more turned to Clough – this time Brian's son, Nigel. For the past 11 years the former Nottingham Forest and England forward had been managing Burton Albion, now on the brink of promotion to the Football League. From Burton, Clough brought with him backroom staff that included Andy Garner, a Rams centre-forward in the Arthur Cox days, and former Forest midfielder Gary Crosby. Another former Forest player, Johnny Metgod, would join the Rams' coaching staff later. Clough soon made his first player signing – centre-forward Chris Porter from Motherwell for £400,000. The loan of Charlton Athletic striker Luke Varney, a Jewell signing, became permanent for £1 million. Neither was to achieve much at Derby. Porter soon struggled with a hip injury; Varney quickly fell out of favour.

The Rams lost Nigel's first two games in charge, but then a run of 13 matches – including four consecutive victories and only three losses – took them up the table before three consecutive defeats in mid-April meant that survival wasn't guaranteed until the penultimate game. The Rams finished 18th, the same as in Brian's first season, but this time few supporters expected football miracles to follow.

Nigel Clough said that the squad contained "too many players", and as the season concluded he began to trim it, with 17 players ultimately leaving Pride Park. One already brought back into the fold, however, was Robbie Savage, exiled by Jewell to Brighton on loan. Clough not only made Savage first choice in the Rams' central midfield, but also organised an extension to the player's contract. Football supporters need a pantomime villain, and Savage had fitted the role perfectly. But now he was a Pride Park favourite. It was a canny – and sensible – piece of self-reinvention.

The major summer signing was Blackpool's centre-half, Shaun Barker, for £900,000. Midfielder Dean Moxey came from Exeter City, for £300,000, and those arriving on free transfers included centre-half Jake

Buxton from Burton Albion, and midfielder Lee Croft from Norwich City. In 2009-10 there were also 14 loan signings, and during the season the Rams used a club record 40 players. Yet at Ipswich in late October, Derby were unable to name their full complement of substitutes. Typical of their bad luck with injuries was reserve goalkeeper Saul Deeney, another close-season signing from Burton Albion, spraining his ankle when slipping in the rain during an unexpected fire drill at the team's hotel for the match at Swansea. Deeney was out for six weeks. By the end of October, in 19th place, the Rams had 16 players on the injury list and Clough considered applying to have matches postponed.

The Rams spent only six matches in the top half of the table, and they were often as low as 20th. By February, though, form began to improve with only one defeat in six matches. March saw a remarkable game at Reading. Shortly after the Rams conceded a goal, Bywater sustained a back injury and was replaced by Deeney who thus made his Football League debut. The Rams equalised through Gilles Sunu, on loan from Arsenal. Then Reading retook the lead. Deeney gave away a 41st-minute penalty and was sent off. Savage took over in goal but although Reading missed the spot-kick they scored twice in the second half to win 4-1. The Rams finished 14th, Championship safety confirmed on 17 April with a 1-1 draw at Selhurst Park.

There was another run to the fifth round of the FA Cup, but perhaps the 2009-10 season is best remembered for incidents off the pitch – or in one instance, nearly off the pitch. At the City Ground on 29 August, Forest's Nathan Tyson marked a hot-tempered 3-2 victory with some animated celebrations with a corner-flag in front of visiting Rams supporters. Tyson was charged with improper conduct, and after the ugly melee that followed his victory jig, both teams were fined for failing to control their players.

When the teams met at Pride Park on 30 January there was more controversy. The Rams won 1-0, and in stoppage time there was another melee in reaction to a push by Chris Gunter on Jay McEveley as the Derby player tried to take a throw-in. After the game Billy Davies accused Clough of "kneeing" him from behind during the incident. "He tried to claim it was an accident but he knows, as well as I know, that it was no accident," claimed Davies, adding: "If he's happy to sit on an electric chair and tell a truth or a lie then I'm happy to sit on an electric chair and we'll see what the outcome is, because I've got no doubt in my mind what happened."

When asked to respond to Davies's allegation, Clough said: "Thanks for the opportunity but I have nothing to say", although he later commented that if there were any contact it must have been accidental: "It was just a melee with arms and legs flying. There were that many bodies in there." Despite Davies's assertion that the matter was in the hands of his lawyers, nothing more was heard of the affair.

Altogether in 2009-10, after three charges of failing to control their players, the Rams paid fines totalling £115,000. When McEveley was sent off for two yellow cards against Swansea – another altercation had occurred after a dreadful tackle on Savage by the Spaniard, Gorka Pintado (who was also dismissed) – he was fined £2,500 but the players, led by Savage, and the management, paid the fine for him. Presumably no one had a whip-round when manager Clough was fined £1,000 and given a one-match touchline ban after being sent to the stands during the match against Ipswich Town on Easter Monday. Pearson was also sent off in that match – the Rams were earning themselves a bit of a reputation ...

In January, after the Rams lost 4-1 at home to Scunthorpe United, there was a verbal "scuffle" between the Rams skipper, Robbie Savage, and BBC Radio Derby's Colin Gibson, who suggested that some Rams' players were dissatisfied with several of Clough's backroom staff. Live on air, an outraged Savage denied the insinuation and accused the radio station of having a vendetta against the club: "The backroom staff are up to the job, no question in my mind, or in the mind of any of the players. I've never heard one player question the manager or somebody[Metgod] who's played for Real Madrid, or somebody who's played in the Premier League ... "

The summer of 2010 was a hive of activity at Pride Park. At the end of August the long-awaited Clough/Taylor statue was unveiled outside the stadium. Standing some 9ft high, it showed the pair holding the Football League Championship trophy. Supporters loved it but were perhaps more diverted by speculation that continued to surround Rob Hulse. In June chief executive Tom Glick had told BBC Radio Derby: "We're not in a position where we need to sell Rob." But on 31 August, QPR swooped in with a £500,000 fee – or £750,000 that could rise to £1 million, it depended on which newspaper you read. Whichever, Hulse, scorer of 28 goals in 82 league appearances for the Rams, had gone.

Incoming players included defenders John Brayford from Crewe Alexandra and Gareth Roberts (Doncaster Rovers), midfielders James

Bailey (Crewe), Ben Davies (Notts County) and Dave Martin (Millwall), and forwards Thomas Cywka (Wigan Athletic) and Conor Doyle from US collegiate soccer. In January the Rams paid Notts County £350,000 for midfielder Ben Davies. During the season another dozen loan players arrived including goalkeeper Frank Fielding from Blackburn, and forwards Jamie Ward (Sheffield United) and Theo Robinson (Millwall). Robinson divided opinion. He had undeniably blistering pace but sometimes looked quite hapless when clear on goal. Clough was also having another clearout. Connelly, McEveley and Teale were among those released before the season began. Commons (to Celtic, £300,000) and Moxey (Palace, £400,000) were sold in January, and the recently signed Martin was off to Notts County on a three-month loan.

The Rams made a poor start – four points from their first four matches – before eight wins in 11 games lifted them into the play-off positions. But the next 28 matches brought only four victories, and a 19th-place finish not confirmed until the 44th game of the season. The Rams even lost that – 3-2 at Norwich – but results elsewhere went their way. Derby's 49 points was their lowest ever total from a 46-game season.

Against a background of growing dissatisfaction among supporters, Peter Gadsby announced that he wanted "to be involved with the club again". The board confirmed that they had received a letter written on behalf of Gadsby, but that no specific information on the manner of his proposed involvement had been included.

Attendances at Pride Park had started to drop slightly – although Derby County were still the third-best supported club in the Championship – and confidence was slipping too. Of the Pride Park faithful, Robbie Savage told the press: "What you want them to do, when we are not playing well, is get behind us. It's as if they're waiting for a mistake to get on our backs." In truth the fans were still suffering from that record-breaking worst-ever season. The emotional impact of that still stung and every small reverse was perhaps felt more keenly than it might ordinarily have been. A shock exit in the third round of the FA Cup to non-League Crawley Town hadn't helped, although it did elicit an apology from Clough: "I acknowledge that it has embarrassed our supporters and for that are very sorry. This apology isn't just for the fantastic travelling support who made the journey yesterday to see us lose, but also the thousands of Derby County supporters who care passionately about this club." And when asked about supporters booing the players after a

3-1 home defeat by Doncaster in March, Clough replied: "I thought they should have booed a little louder." As for the chants of "You don't know what you're doing!" directed at the manager after his substitution of Theo Robinson: "They are entitled to do that." PFA chief Gordon Taylor took exception to the manager's public criticism of Thomas Cywka who, after a 1-1 draw at Portsmouth, was described by Clough as "extremely inexperienced" and "a not very bright footballer ... he can go back to Wigan or wherever he came from – I'm not really bothered – until he learns the game." Taylor said that not only was such public criticism inappropriate, but that it could also lead to "an untenable situation". One doubts that Clough took much notice.

As the season came to a close Fielding, Robinson and Ward were signed on permanent deals, but Robbie Savage confirmed that, after 623 senior club appearances in English football, he was retiring as a player. In his last two games, a home defeat by Bristol City and an away loss at Reading, he was given a standing ovation by both sets of supporters. Who would have thought it?

In the 2011 close season there were more comings and goings. The Rams paid Barnsley £750,000 for their centre-half Jason Shackell, £400,000 to Aberdeen for striker Chris Maguire, and £350,000 to Kilmarnock for midfielder Craig Bryson, while the corner-flag-waving Nathan Tyson came to Pride Park on a free transfer from Nottingham Forest, probably thinking: "Well, if Robbie Savage can come here and leave a hero, so can I." It didn't quite work out like that, although Rams fans still forgave if they didn't actually forget. Burton Albion goalkeeper Adam Legzdins arrived for an undisclosed fee, and former Rams centre-half Chris Riggott returned to Pride Park to see if he could regain his fitness sufficiently to carry on as a Football League player. Riggott, plagued by injuries in recent years, had undergone surgery on a back problem in April. Niggling Achilles' tendon, calf and back injuries had hindered him in his second spell at Derby, and in December his contract was cancelled by mutual consent.

Out of Pride Park also went Varney (sold to Portsmouth for £750,000) and Porter (released at the end of his contract) to be followed in due course by others including Pearson, Martin, Dean Leacock, Cywka, and Stephen Bywater who had upset his Derbyshire neighbours with an "art installation" – a decorated portable toilet and horse box complete with two inflatable sex toys – in his garden but visible from the street. A tarpaulin was used to good effect and the goalkeeper apologised for any offence caused. And we used to think that Reg Matthews was a bit of a character ...

The Rams started 2011-12 well, winning their first four league games, something they hadn't done since 1905-06 (when they won the first five). A League Cup defeat at the hands of League Two opposition – this time Shrewsbury Town – for the third season in a row was disappointing, but all that was forgotten when the Rams, fourth in the table, went to the City Ground on 17 September and won 2-1 despite having goalkeeper Frank Fielding sent off after only 67 seconds. Former Academy player Jeff Hendrick's winner was his first goal in senior football.

When they travelled to Leicester on 1 October, the Rams stood third in the table. After they lost 4-0, they began to tumble again, down to 15th by the end of November. By mid-January they were back up to eighth, but down to 16th by early March. In the middle of that month, Shaun Barker, who had already been sidelined for a lengthy spell, was taken to hospital after colliding with former Ram, Marcus Tudgay, against Nottingham Forest at Pride Park. Derby's first league double over Forest in 40 years was overshadowed by news that the centre-half had dislocated his kneecap, and ruptured his medial, anterior cruciate and posterior cruciate ligaments. Following surgery to his patellar ligament, it was suggested that he would need at least 16 months to recover,

Fourteen points out of a possible 21 from the start of April prompted the more optimistic supporters to speak of the play-offs. But two home defeats in four days ended such wild dreams. Still, a 12th place finish in the Championship was the Rams' best since relegation in 2008. More pleasing still was the fact that Derby had relied far less on loan signings and more on homegrown talent. Mark O'Brien (who in November 2009 had successfully undergone heart surgery to correct a valve problem), Jeff Hendrick, Callum Ball, Mason Bennett and Will Hughes had all made a mark, with Bennett setting a club record as the youngest ever Rams' first-team player when he made his debut against Middlesbrough on 22 October 2011. At 15 years and 99 days, he beat Lee Holmes's record by 169 days. Bennett had been considered for the midweek game at Reading but Clough said: "We'd only get back from Reading at about 2am on Wednesday and he had school that morning." On 5 January 2013, Bennett would take another record from Holmes: in the 5-0 FA Cup third-round win over League One Tranmere Rovers that day, Bennett's goal made him

– at 16 years and 174 days – the youngest-ever scorer in Derby County's history.

With Shaun Barker certain to miss the entire season, there was great surprise in the summer of 2012 when the Rams eventually accepted a £1.1 million bid from Burnley for Jason Shackell. It left them a without an established centre-half to partner Barker, but Clough acted swiftly, bringing in Coventry City's Richard Keogh for £1 million. The squad was forever changing. A long-time Clough target, centre-forward Conor Sammon, was signed from Wigan Athletic for £1.2 million. Midfielders Michael Jacobs (from Northampton Town for an undisclosed fee) and Paul Coutts (from Preston for £150,000) came in. And after Christmas, Norwich City striker Chris Martin, and Watford left-back or left midfielder Craig Forsyth both joined Derby on loan.

Jamie Ward signed a contract extension, but despite the club's attempts to secure him to a new contract Paul Green decided to move on. Maguire went to Sheffield Wednesday for £200,000, Steve Davies, the Rams' leading league scorer in 2011-12, moved to Bristol City for £750,000 in the January transfer window, and there were loan transfers for Robinson (12 goals in all games in 2011-12) to Huddersfield Town, Tyson to Millwall, Croft to Oldham Athletic, and Bailey and former Academy scholar Callum Ball both to Coventry City. Miles Addison – of whom great things had been expected but had never materialised after a succession of foot problems saw him undergo specialist surgery in the USA – was also allowed to leave. Nigel Clough summed up 2012-13 as a season in which Derby County were "frustratingly close to the top six". At Elland Road on Easter Monday, Buxton scored an 88th-minute winner to ensure that the Rams' winning streak over Leeds United extended to nine games and move Derby up to eighth, six points from the play-off places. But they could win only two of their remaining six matches to finish 10th.

Overall, Nigel Clough has overseen inch-by-inch progress at Pride Park, which seems to suit the club's American owners who have so far displayed only modest ambition. The fans, of course, feel that Derby County Football Club, with its amazing supporters, fine tradition, splendid stadium and state-of-the-art training complex, has the potential for so much more. They are right, of course. If Steve Bloomer really is watching, he must be getting restless.